The Barbecue Cookbook

Arto der Haroutunian is now a British citizen but was born in Aleppo, Syria in 1940. His father's family were from Southern Turkey and his mother's from Armenia. He took a degree in architecture at Manchester University and has been a practising architect ever since, specializing in designing restaurants, clubs and hotels.

In 1970, in partnership with his brother, he opened the first Armenian restaurant in Manchester, which has developed today into a successful chain of restaurants and hotels. As well as his passion for cooking. Arto der Haroutunian is a painter of international reputation who has exhibited all over the world. His other interests include composing music and translating Turkish, Arab, Persian and Armenian authors. He lives in Cheshire with his wife and son.

His book *Middle Eastern Cookery* is also available in Pan.

The Barbecue Cookbook

Arto der Haroutunian

Pan Books London and Sydney

First published 1986 by Pan Books Ltd,
Cavaye Place, London, SW10 9PG
9 8 7 6 5 4 3 2 1
© Arto der Haroutunian 1986
Illustrations © Andrew Macdonald 1986
ISBN 0 330 29188 2

Phototypeset by Input Typesetting Ltd, London SW19 8DR
Printed by Cox & Wyman Ltd, Reading, Berks RG1 8EX

Contents

Introduction

Where light is admitted, darkness is driven away – Zoroaster

Cooking over a wood or charcoal fire dates back to the dawn of our civilization. The accredited home of this form of cooking is reputed to be the Caucasus – the high mountain ranges with their impressive towering peaks and deep valleys – that lie between the Black and Caspian Seas. It was here that Prometheus brought fire (stolen from Heaven), carried in the hollow stalk of a fennel plant and gave it to Mankind.

By the shores of Lake Van (Turkish Armenia) both the Hurrian and the Urartian fire-worshipping empires flourished; and around 100BC Zoroaster and his followers compiled the great religio-social compendium the *Avesta* where God was symbolized by the perpetually burning sacred fire – a representation of the immortality of Good over Evil, Light over Dark.

This area was the cradle of our western civilization where plants and animals were first cultivated and domesticated, enabling man to live in permanent settlements and create a truly agricultural society. At sundown the flock of sheep was herded back to the settlement and one or two of the best horned rams were picked out for food. With a sharp-edged knife the shepherd slit the skin of the animal and pulled the body through the small opening. The intestines were removed, the animal washed and the cavity filled with wheat, vegetables, nuts and dried fruits. The animal was then returned to the skin. A pit was dug, usually about 1.8m (6ft) deep and about 1m (3ft 3in) square. A bed of wood was laid at the bottom of the pit, lit and left until the flames subsided and the wood was glowing. The animal was then laid lengthways in the pit, the spaces were filled in with earth or mud and the top of the pit covered. Six hours later the animal was removed, brushed to pluck away the soil clinging to the skin and then placed on a large tray. The elders of the settlement blessed the meat and the festivities commenced.

This method of cooking is still popular in places as far apart as Anatolia, Central Africa and Australia.

In time this very primitive method was replaced by stone and metal grills. The first known grills to have been found were shallow pits from the Neolithic settlement of Medzamor (Armenia) – 6000BC, Knossos (Crete) – 5000BC, Northern India and Jarmo (North Iraq) – 6000–5000BC. They all had the same basic construction i.e. a shallow pit in the ground – some were round as at Medzamor while others were rectangular. Wide heavy stones were deposited on all sides to hold the long logs along which the animal was positioned. Wood was the first source of heat used, but gorse sticks, old turves and dried heather roots were all used for a good consistent fire. Normally the fire was kept burning and it was the duty of a member of the settlement to see to its upkeep. Over the years wood was replaced by charcoal – a more practical and economic form of heating, which in the early stages was considered a useless by-product of the iron and copper smelting of the Hittite and Urartian empires. The ores were placed in deep pits, covered with wood, which in turn was overlaid with ash and earth to stop the heat being lost. The melted ore would flow through specially made channels. During the process a certain amount of wood turned into charcoal – the qualities of which were soon discovered.

In Medieval Britain and in Europe generally animals, whole or in part, were spit-roasted. The spit rested on an iron 'dog' at each end of the hearth and was turned from one end by a cook-boy. The spits were made of wrought iron with a claw-shaped prong. There were also very thin 'bird spits' on which several little birds were strung.

Essentially outdoor fare, food cooked over charcoal was

naturally more popular in warmer climates and especially
among nomadic societies – people constantly on the move
and hence restricted with time and utensils. Thus it
retained its prominence in the Middle Eastern and North
Indian cuisines while it virtually disappeared from the more
urbanized and industrialized ones of western Europe. That
is, until a few decades ago when it was resurrected to its
former prominence in the USA, particularly in sun-drenched
California and, like most 'born again' concepts, it has
become a fashionable way of eating – indeed, almost a way
of life!

In recent years, in spite of unpredictable weather and
centuries-held reluctance to cook and eat outdoors, the
British are gradually beginning to appreciate the many
faceted qualities of outdoor cookery. For there is nothing
like the wonderful taste of meat, fish, poultry or vegetables
grilled over wood or charcoal, or their marvellous aroma as it
drifts up to the leaves and beyond. Understandably therefore
barbecuing is becoming increasingly popular for it is easy
to prepare, not very time consuming and most enjoyable.

The word 'barbecue' is derived from the Spanish *barbacoa*
– the frame on which the American Indians used to cook
their meats. In other parts of the world meat grilled over
wood or charcoal is called 'kebab' (or 'kabob' or 'kobob') from
the classic Persian *kabab* meaning 'to burn'. From the outset
it is important to note the subtle difference between these
two cooking methods. 'Kebab' today has come to mean pieces
of meat, poultry or fish marinated for 8–12 hours in oil and
spices, small enough to be threaded onto skewers (wood or
metal), but large enough not to fall off into the fire and
disintegrate. 'Barbecue' on the other hand refers to any cut
of meat (steaks, chops, sausages, burgers etc), not
necessarily marinated but often basted with oil or butter.

I have found that there is a geographical area where kebab
dishes predominate. It stretches along the eastern shores of
the Mediterranean i.e. Greece and Cyprus, skirting the North
African coast to the Middle East in general then through
Turkey, Iran, the Caucasus and down to the Indian sub-
continent. The satés of Indonesia and Malaysia were

probably introduced by the incoming Muslims who brought
with them the cultural and socio-economic customs of Arab-
Persian Islam. Indeed it is Islam that has, for the past
fourteen centuries dominated the whole of the 'kebab area'
as, with the exception of the Christian Greeks, Georgians,
Maronite Lebanese and Armenians the rest of the populace
are Muslims. When the empire of the Arabs collapsed and
was replaced by that of the Mongolian-Turks 'kebabs' made
their appearance in the Balkans – Yugoslavia, Romania and
Bulgaria – and in Southern Italy. Lamb predominates in
these lands. There are few beef dishes, some poultry and no
pork whatsoever save in the Christian regions such as the
Balkans, Greece and the Caucasus.

Further afield in Europe and North America it is beef that
predominates. An exciting culinary area is the Caribbean
where Indian, African and European cultures have
intermingled to create a rich, though sometimes over-
burdened cuisine. Unfortunately I have not included several
interesting recipes from this area because of the lack of
availability of some ingredients. Nor have I dared to include
'shark kebab' or 'turtle steak kebab'!

I have found very few kebabs in South America interesting
enough for inclusion although a few from Mexico merit
attention for their clever use of hot peppers. The Far East –
China, Japan and Korea – have a school of kebabs of their
own. They are normally beef with marinades of soy sauce,
mirin, saké, ginger etc.

This book is about barbecues and kebabs from all over the
world with all the appropriate accompaniments of rice and
other grains, salads, vegetables and breads. Some of them
use exotic and unfamiliar spices and ingredients. The
Glossary on p. 254 explains what these are and where you
may be able to buy them, though often I have suggested a
more easily available substitute in the recipe itself.

Good cooking and *Bon Appetit*!

Choosing the grill

'What is Heaven on the outside
And Hell in the centre? – Fire.' – *Armenian saying*

The first requirement for barbecueing is a grill. Over recent
years, no doubt influenced by the American love of barbecue
picnics or parties, many commercial companies have
marketed barbecues – steel or iron utensils with a charcoal
fire receptacle. The food is cooked on a metal grid or on
skewers.

The ideal place for a barbecue is in a sheltered part of the
garden, near the kitchen, but most certainly away from all
shrubbery and flower beds. Having chosen the grill's position
you are now faced with a much more difficult problem – that
of choosing the type of grill. If, like me, you like to eat out
of doors whenever given the chance then you could make
your grill a permanent feature of the garden. Build a brick
one similar to those illustrated with good solid foundations,
preferably bedded on 15cm (6in) concrete. Pave the
surrounding area – this is hygienic, attractive and practical
since you can put out a table and chairs and eat in comfort.
The design and construction of a brick-built barbecue will
primarily depend on how much you wish to spend. The
simplest grill need not be any more elaborate than the
sketches that follow. A slightly more elaborate barbecue
could incorporate storage space for charcoal or wood, a
serving area and space to hang a large spit for a whole
chicken, turkey or even a small lamb or pig.

With a little more expense you could install a Tonir – a
brick-lined outdoor oven which resembles the clay 'Tandoori
ovens' of Northern India. The standard tonir has a shallow

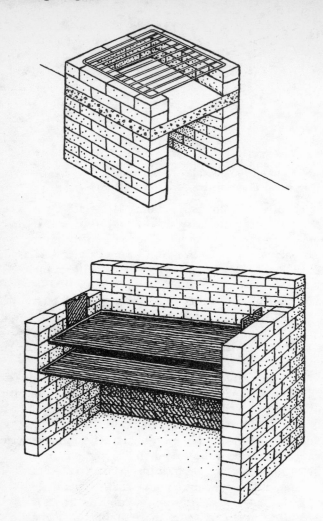

well about 60cm (2 ft) across and 1.20m (4 ft) deep partly
set below ground. A wooden platform surrounds the open top.
As with the tandoori oven a tonir is used both for grilling
cuts of meat and poultry on long metal skewers and for
baking bread e.g. *nan* or *lavash*.

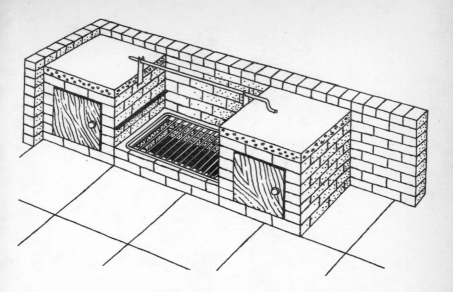

You can, of course always improvise and prepare quick and
efficient grills out of biscuit tins, large tin cans, timber
planks, large stones etc. After all on-the-spot improvisation
and a general air of informality are two of the more
attractive aspects of barbecuing.

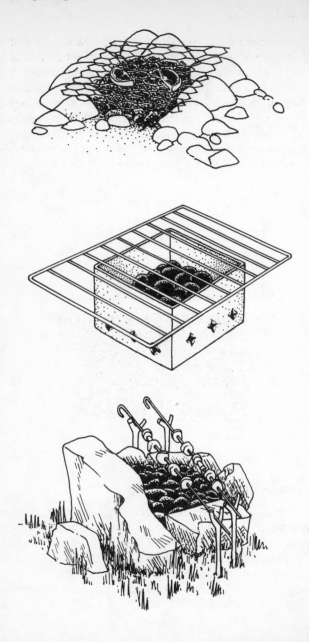

Indoor grill

Although barbecuing is usually regarded as an outdoor
activity there are no major impediments if you wish to cook
indoors as long as the awkward problem of ventilation is
carefully thought out. Both charcoal and wood will give off
fumes (carbon monoxide) and there is also the problem of the
lingering odour of meat, particularly that of minced meat
whose fat drips on to the charcoal. The ideal place then must
be the fireplace whose chimney will disperse all the fumes
and unwanted odours. The fireplace can thus be treated as a
fire-box.

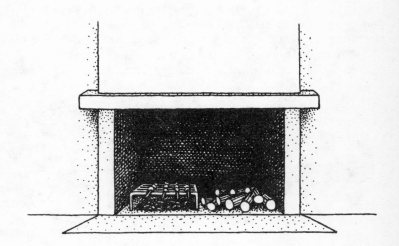

Ready-made barbecues

Probably the most convenient barbecues for everyday cooking
are those purpose-made ones which are readily available in
the shops, stores and even some petrol stations. They are, for
the most part made of aluminium or stainless steel. The
choice is wide and prices vary from a few pounds to hundreds.
The more traditional ones are the heavy metal 'Hibachis'
or the Mexican 'Braseros'. *Hibachi* – a word which means

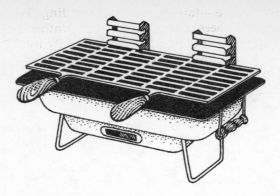

'fire-box' in Japanese where it first originated. It is now widely used throughout the world for it is both simple to operate and reasonable in price. Hibachis are usually made of cast iron with wooden handles and base. The grills have adjustable levels to allow for draught control. There are two

types available – table top or free standing. The one drawback of these grills is their size – rather small; perhaps ideal for the average family, but certainly inadequate for large parties. However, all is not lost for in recent years both 'double' and 'triple' hibachis have been arriving in our country all the way from the Land of the Rising Sun!

Braseros (Braziers) The traditional Braseros come in terracotta or black Oaxacan pottery. They are not only practical but aesthetically pleasing. Braseros are, as yet, not easily available. Of those that are, by far the most popular are those small, round portable barbecues which have revolving grills and are sometimes hooded. The more expensive ones also come with spits. They do vary in size from 45cm (18in) to 60cm (2ft) and over; they can also come with an additional work surface or clip-on tray – very useful, particularly when cooking for a large number of people.

However, the final choice will depend upon a) how often (weather permitting perhaps) you intend to use your barbecue grill and b) how much you wish to spend when purchasing one.

If, for you, money is no object then there is the 'Wagon Grill'. This is a large covered barbecue mounted on wheels. It is usually rectangular in shape although cylindrical models are also available. This type of grill usually has built-in storage cabinets, oven temperature gauge, motorised spits and is made of high-grade steel with enamelled store.

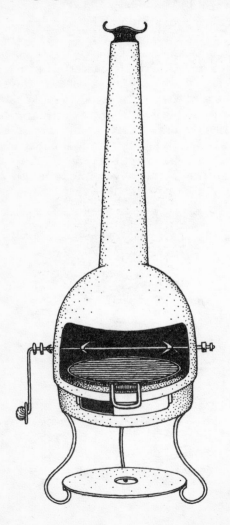

Certain makes even have tall funnels which help to stop the draught, keep the charcoal glowing and prevent smoke going all over the garden. Some models also have a separate access door to the fire.

Gas and electric barbecues

In these charcoal is substituted with natural lava or a similar man-made product. When heated by the electric or gas element the rock emits a radiant heat, the level of which can be controlled by the turn of a knob.

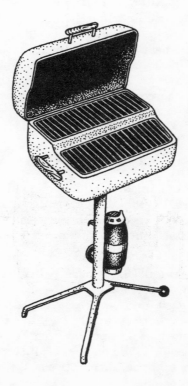

However, purely on a personal level, I do not regard these as true barbecues as they lack the most essential ingredient – genuine charcoal. On the other hand I must admit that they are clean, cheaper to run and hence more economical than charcoal barbecues.

Preparing the fire

'He was a poor charcoal-burner and lived in the forest deep.' – *Fairytale.*

As with a permanent brick-built barbecue, a ready-made grill should also be located in a safe place i.e. away from trees, bushes and fences. Also check the wind direction – you would not wish all the fumes and odours to penetrate your or your neighbour's house! After you have found the best location for the grill I suggest you first line the fire bowl with aluminium foil – shiny side out – this will both aid cleaning up and reflect the heat back on to the food, thus speeding up the cooking time. Next spread a layer of clean dry gravel or sand (about ½–1cm (¼–½in) thick over the foil. This will support the charcoal and permit air to pass under and through it, causing it to burn evenly. The gravel can be washed, dried and re-used.

Fuel

Although it is quite acceptable to use wood in ready-made barbecues, charcoal is the fuel I strongly recommend. It comes either as lumpwood or as briquettes. It is slow burning and generates intense heat. A few words then about charcoal.

Lumpwood charcoal This is usually made from softwood (cedar, pine, ash, larch, hawthorn etc), though hardwood is sometimes also used. Lumpwood charcoal is produced by the age-old method of charring wood in a kiln. It is sold in varying sizes – most of it imported from Europe. It ignites well but burns faster than charcoal briquettes. Lumpwood charcoal has two other characteristics a) it gives up sparks

– so do take care not to stray too near the fire and b) it gives a slight flavour to the food. Although this latter characteristic may not please some people, I believe it enhances the flavour of the cooked food. Indeed, many Middle Eastern and Indian cooks throw herbs and spices into the glowing embers of the fire to further enrich the aroma and taste of the food.

Charcoal briquettes Charcoal in briquette form is usually made from hardwood (beech, oak, birch etc). The briquettes burn for a long time and emit little smoke or odour as they have a lower resin content than softwood charcoal. The briquettes produce an intense and even heat and have become more popular than their lumpwood counterparts.

Mineral briquettes These are made from mineral carbons which are pulverized and then bound with starch into 5cm (2in) round briquettes which glow and do not flame and which produce a good, consistent heat. They are much used in the catering industry, producing all those insipid 'char-grilled' burgers and sausages.

How much charcoal

The amount of charcoal needed will naturally differ with the size of your barbecue and the amount of food to be cooked. Steaks, chops, minced meat, burgers and sausages need less time and charcoal than larger roasts of leg of lamb, fowl or game.

Do not build too large a fire – a tendency of many ambitious beginner chefs! Estimate your needs and then proceed, but remember that there is no need to make a large fire over the whole grill area; rest assured that after a few attempts you will get the charcoal to food proportions right.

Wood A wood fire takes much longer to burn down to a bed of coals, so start about 2 hours before cooking time. Use wood only when out in the country on a picnic or if there is plenty of wood available nearby. Or for large barbecues and pit-cooking such as for a whole lamb (page 58) or suckling

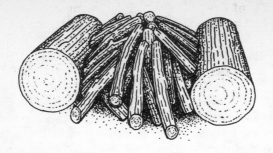

pig (page 105). Though any wood will do, I suggest a hardwood such as oak, beech, ash, yew, holly, cherry, pear etc. There are many types of wood fire for outdoor cooking. My favourite is 'Hunter's Fire'. Logs or bricks are laid on either side of wood, which should be arranged over firelighters or crumpled paper in the form of a wigwam. Once the sticks of wood are burning start adding larger pieces until the fire is going well and is maintained along the whole length of the logs or bricks. The logs or bricks retain the heat of the fire as well as reflecting it inwards to improve its efficiency.

Lighting the fire

First a word of warning – NEVER use petrol or other volatile fuels such as paraffin, naphtha etc. They are not only DANGEROUS, but will ruin the flavour of the food.

White block firelighter These small white blocks are the best. They are cheap, efficient and easily available from ironmongers. Break off 2–3 pieces and place them inside the charcoal pyramid. After lighting, the starter will burn for 10–15 minutes and the fire should then be ready for cooking in 20–30 minutes. These white block starters are also available in granulated form. If using this type I suggest you sprinkle the charcoal pyramid with granules. Light them at 4–5 points. After 20–30 minutes the fire will be ready for cooking.

Other types of firelighters The following are also available:
(a) self-lighting charcoal. This is specially treated briquettes
which are rather expensive. Place 4–5 briquettes on the fire
bed and light. The fire should be ready in 40 minutes.
(b) Liquid fire starter. Arrange the charcoal pyramid, pour
the liquid over, wait 3–4 minutes for the liquid to soak in
and then light the charcoal with a taper. The fire should be
ready in about 30 minutes. For safety's sake follow the
manufacturer's instructions most carefully.

Electric fire starters and jellied alcohol can also be used to
start a fire.

I do not recommend the use of a gas torch or blow lamp
although I know that many people do resort to them.

Controlling the fire

In time you should be able to 'understand' the heat
requirement of your barbecue fire-box, but until then a few
hints.
(a) Light the fire well in advance – 30 minutes for charcoal
and 2 hours for wood. When the charcoal is well and truly
lit and the flames have died down, spread the glowing coals
evenly over the base of the grill. Keep extra coal around
the edge ready to push into the centre if needed.
(b) To increase the heat, lower the grill nearer to the fire or
raise the fire-box if it is adjustable. Open the draughts in your
barbecue (if any) to let more air through. You can of course
add more coal, but use charcoal that has been warmed
around the edge of the fire first.
(c) To reduce the heat either lower the fire-box, raise the
height of the grill or close the draughts.

Note: **do not cook food over flames or thick smoke – all
you will get will be charred food**.

After cooking

When you have finished cooking, extinguish the fire with old
cinders or a very fine water-spray. If your barbecue has a

hood, lower it and shut the dampers – the fire will slowly be snuffed out.

A word of caution – **Never** douse the fire with water. Instead use tongs or a small shovel to transfer the coals to a metal bucket and then sprinkle with water.

In a similar spirit of safety-first, I strongly recommend that you have a first-aid kit available for all the unexpected accidents that may occur. Make sure that the kit includes an ointment or spray for burns, plasters for cuts, antiseptic, cotton wool etc.

Have a pleasant and safe barbecue!

Accessories

Long tongs – one pair for lifting and turning food and one pair for the charcoal.
Oven gloves – absolutely indispensable.
Bellows – if not available then improvise with a stiff piece of cardboard that can be used as a fan.
Brush – for basting. Use pure bristle and NEVER bristle-type, man-made fibre as this is highly inflammable.

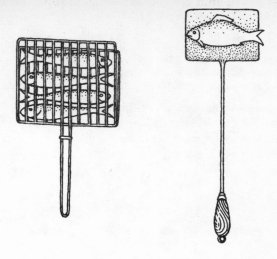

Spoons and forks – use long handled ones with wooden grips.
Hinged wire grill – ideal for fish. This grill has long handles
and can be easily turned.
Aluminium foil – a heavy duty foil is good for keeping the
food clean and warm.
Skewers – these can be bought at almost any ironmongers.
Choose long, flat ones rather than round ones so that the
meat will not slip when the skewers are turned. If possible
buy ones with wooden handles as these do not get too hot
to handle! Two-pronged skewers can be used for holding
larger pieces of meat or poultry.

Before cooking check this list

Whether your barbecue is just for a few people or for a large
party I strongly recommend you check this list to ensure
that all the necessary items are at hand. There is nothing
worse than to have to keep dashing to the kitchen for this
or that.

Salt, pepper and various herbs and spices according to taste.
Sharp knives for carving.
Meat thermometer if cooking a large piece of meat.
A large work surface near the grill – a table perhaps with heatproof
  mats to prevent singeing
Fireproof bowls for bastes and marinades.
Plates and cutlery.

And of course salads and vegetables, baskets full of bread,
glasses, ice bucket and bottle opener, plenty of paper
napkins **and** a large waste bin!

Cooking methods

1 On the grill

Before placing the meat on a grill brush the latter with a
little oil to prevent the food (this applies particularly to
minced meat) sticking to the hot grid. Open grill cooking is
the most popular method of all barbecue cooking. It is
excellent for steaks, chops, sausages, chicken and other fowl
pieces and fish. I strongly recommend that you marinate all
your meat, preferably for several hours. Food just basted will
never be as flavoursome as marinated food because the
flavour of the baste will only cling to the surface. So marinate
whenever possible as the flavour will permeate the meat.

  When cooking place the meat on the grill and place about
7.5cm (3in) above the fire. This will sear the meat and help
to preserve the juices. Then raise the grill until about
10–12.5cm (4–5in) above the fire. For a guide to cooking
times see pages 30–32.

2 On skewers

This is undoubtably the oldest method of cooking on fire.
Thin metal or wooden sticks are threaded with marinated
chunks of meat, fish or chicken and cooked over charcoal. If
you pack the meat tightly together it will take longer to
cook and the centres of the chunks of meat will be tender
and juicy. For cooking times see chart pages 30–32, but do
bear in mind that you must have no flames nor should the
fire be too hot. Beware also of the occasional 'flare-up' from
fat dripping on to the hot coals.

Although you can baste skewered food I suggest that you
marinate the pieces first as the flavour will be so much
better. As well as meat, fish, chicken etc you can also skewer
and grill fruits and vegetables with great success. Skewered
barbecues are – in my opinion – the finest and most
sophisticated form of cooking and consequently I have
included a great many such recipes in this book.

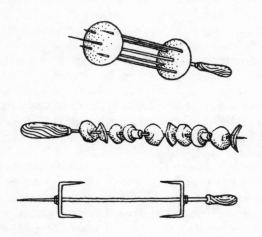

3 On the spit

Spit cooking is the only true form of roasting (oven 'roasting'
is in reality more of a bake). Spit cooking is excellent for
leg of lamb, large fish, poultry and loin of pork. The food's
juices and bastes roll around the surface as the spit turns,
rather than drip off into a pan or into the fire; thus the meat
stays moist and flavoursome since it bastes itself. Many
barbecues incorporate rotisserie equipment, but if your grill
lacks this you can easily attach a spit to it – the latter
comes in many forms. For practical purposes the spit should

be an electric or battery powered type. A good spit, usually made of steel, is 0.5cm (¼in) square with two forks. Each fork should have four tines which pierce and hold the meat firmly.

The only problem with spit cooking is the balancing of the meat. It is important that the spit turns evenly without any jerks, fits and starts; otherwise the meat will be unevenly cooked. To achieve the correct balance I suggest the following simple test. Hold the spit in the palms of your hands, then slowly rotate. If you feel it rolling quickly from any position then it means the spit is unbalanced. Therefore re-skewer the meat and test once again. If these changes in balance occur during cooking (more common with fatty meat) use a balancing weight or respit the meat.

The easiest roasts to balance are those of uniform texture and shape. Small birds are fairly easy to grill too. Truss them firmly so that the wings and drumsticks stay close to the body.

Various barbecue accessories are available for use with the spit eg spit baskets made of wire – either in flat or cylindrical form and a 'shish kebab' attachment which enables you to cook several skewers of kebabs at the same time. Indeed, although the spit is best for large chunks of meat or poultry you can roast almost anything with it – if carefully prepared.

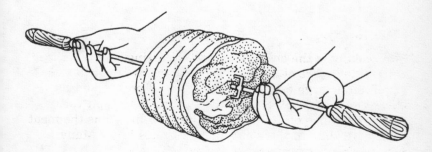

Grilling time chart

Variety of meat	Cut of meat	Size/weight	Fire heat	Approximate cooking time each side		
				Rare	Medium	Well done
Lamb	chops or steak	2.5cm (1in) thick	medium	5–6min	7–8min	10–11min
	skewer	–	medium	5–6min	7–8min	10–11min
Beef	steak	2.5cm (1in) thick	hot	5–6min	7–8min	10–12min
	steak	3.5cm (1½in) thick	hot	6–7min	9–10min	12–15min
	hamburger	2.5cm (1in)	medium	4min	5–6min	7–9min
	skewer	–	hot	5–6min	7–8min	10–12min
Pork	chops	2.5cm (1in) thick	medium	–	–	15–18min
	sausages	individual	medium	–	–	8–10min
	skewers	–	medium	–	–	15–18min
Poultry	chicken	split	medium	–	–	20–25min
		portion	medium	–	–	15–20min
	duck	split	medium	–	–	25min
	turkey	portion	medium	–	–	25min
	pheasant	portion	medium	–	–	20–25min
Veal	steak or chops	2.5cm (1in) thick	medium	–	–	10–12min
	skewer	–	medium	–	–	12–15min

Venison	steak or chops	2.5cm (1in) thick	medium	–	–	10–12min
Fish	steak	1cm (½in)	medium	–	–	3–4min
	steak	2.5cm (1in)	medium	–	–	5–7min
	whole (small)	450g–575g (1–1¼lb)	medium	–	–	20min
	whole (large)	1–1.25kg (2–2½lb)	medium	–	–	40–45min
	fillets	2cm (¾in)	medium	–	–	5–7min

Spit-roasting time chart

Lamb	leg	1.5–3kg (3½–7lb)	medium	1–1¼hr	1½–2hr	2½–3¼hr
	rolled shoulder	1.5–2.75kg (3½–6½lb)	medium	1–1¼hr	1½–2hr	2½–3¼hr
	kid/baby lamb	3–6kg (7–14lb) or 7–12kg (15–28lb)	low–med	–	–	3½–4½hr

Beef	rump (rolled)	1.5–2.25kg (3–5lb)	medium	1½–2hr	2¼–3hr	3–4hr
	sirloin	2.25–2.75kg (5–6lb)	med–hot	1½–1¾hr	2½–3hr	3–4hr
	rolled rib	1.75–2.75kg (4–6lb)	med–hot	2–2½hr	2½–3hr	3½–4½hr
Pork	shoulder	1.5–2.5kg (3–5lb)	medium	–	–	2–3hr
	loin	1.5–2.5kg (3–5lb)	medium	–	–	2–3hr
	suckling pig	5–6kg (10–12lb)	medium	–	–	3–4hr
Poultry	chicken	1.25–2.25kg (2½–5lb)	medium	–	–	1–1½hr
	turkey	4.5–8kg (10–18lb)	medium	–	–	2–4hr
	duckling	1.75–2.75kg (4–6lb)	medium	–	–	1–2hr
	goose	3.5–6.5kg (8–15lb)	medium	–	–	1–2hr

Comments

1 The degree to which food is cooked will depend on the heat emanating from the charcoal, the distance the food is from the fire and upon the thickness of the meat cuts.

2 Temperatures. These are calculated as follows:

Hot   – 90°C, 190°F
Medium – 70°C, 160°F
Rare   – 60°C, 140°F

For accuracy use a meat thermometer, which should be inserted into the centre of the joint before cooking.

3 To check that the meat is 'done' cut the steak with a sharp knife near the centre.

4 *Lamb* – I do not recommend that lamb be cooked rare. I suggest medium or well-done.

Pork – Should be well-done. Never rare or medium.

Chicken – Should never be over-cooked.

Veal – Should be well-done but never dry.

Venison – Medium-to-rare rather than well-done.

Fish – Never overcook or it will become dry. When fish flakes easily with a fork it is sufficiently cooked.

All recipes are for 6 persons unless otherwise stated.

Starter kebabs

Misket koftesi – marble-sized kebabs

These small, marble-sized kebabs make excellent appetizers.
Do not overcook; 4 to 5 minutes should be enough.

You can serve these kebabs warm or cold. To serve squeeze
some lemon juice over them and sprinkle with a little
paprika.

900g (2lb) lean lamb, minced
2 large onions, coarsely chopped
2 tablespoons chopped parsley
2 teaspoons salt
½ teaspoon black pepper
1 teaspoon cinnamon
40g (1½oz) ghee or melted butter

Garnish
lettuce leaves
lemon wedges
paprika

1 Pass the meat through a mincer together with the onion
and parsley. Place the mixture in a large bowl and season
with the salt, pepper and cinnamon. Knead vigorously for
about 5 minutes until really smooth.
2 Keeping your hands damp with cold water scoop out tiny
portions of the meat mixture and roll each one between your
palms to form marble-sized balls. When all the mixture is
used up thread the balls on to skewers.
3 Cook over charcoal for 4–6 minutes, turning frequently
and brushing with the melted butter or ghee. Remove from

the heat and slide the balls off the skewers on to a serving
plate lined with lettuce leaves.
4 Serve warm or cold with lemon wedges and sprinkle with
a little paprika.

Bari jinga kobob – king prawn kebab

This makes a fine starter. Allow 3–4 large prawns per person.
The large king prawns that are found in most fishmongers are
very appropriate as they, like this recipe, hail from
Bangladesh.

18–24 king prawns, peeled
1 large green pepper, seeded and cut into 2.5cm (1in) squares
1 onion, peeled, quartered and separated into layers

Marinade
1 teaspoon chilli pepper
1 teaspoon curry powder
8 tablespoons olive oil
juice 1 large lemon
½ teaspoon salt

Garnish
lemon wedges

1 First prepare the marinade by mixing all ingredients
together in a bowl. Add the prawns, green pepper and onion
and mix thoroughly. Cover and leave for at least one hour.
2 Thread each skewer with prawns and pieces of onion and
pepper. Cook over charcoal for about 10 minutes turning
occasionally and basting with any remaining marinade.
3 Serve immediately with lemon wedges.

Balal kabab – Corn-on-the-cob kebab

Corn-on-the-cob with rich melted butter has become an
international appetizer but this Middle Eastern recipe
avoids all that fatty content and is, I believe, much more
appetizing. The flavour of charcoal-grilled corn dipped in
salty water (which, according to the Turks should be 'as salty
as sea-water') is superb.

'Balal' or 'Misir' kebab is sold by street vendors throughout the Middle East.

6 ears of corn
1.8l (3 pints) lukewarm water
4–6 tablespoons salt

1 Remove the outer husks from each cob and then strip off the inner husks and all the silk threads.
2 In a large bowl dissolve the salt in the warm water.
3 Place the cobs on the grill and cook over charcoal for 20–25 minutes or until the cobs are lightly and evenly browned and the kernels are puffed up. Turn frequently and take care not to burn.
4 Remove the cobs from the grill and dip them immediately into the salty water for 2–3 seconds. Serve immediately.

Saté – Indonesian kebab

This is a simple saté dish and one of the most popular throughout south-east Asia. The sauce has been simplified slightly to make it more practical. This kebab may be served as a first course, in which case it will serve 8–10 people or with boiled rice as a lunch or dinner dish, in which case it will serve 6.

900g (2lb) boned leg of lamb, cut into 2.5cm (1in) cubes

Marinade
3 cloves garlic, crushed
4 tablespoons soy sauce
1 tablespoon soft brown sugar
1 small onion, grated
1 tablespoon lemon juice
¼ teaspoon salt

Sauce
150ml (5fl oz) soy sauce
1 teaspoon ground coriander
1 clove garlic, crushed
1 green or red chilli, finely chopped
3 tablespoons soft brown sugar

2 tablespoons dark treacle or molasses
1 tablespoon lemon juice

1 Mix the marinade ingredients together in a large bowl.
Add the meat cubes, turn to coat evenly with the marinade,
cover and set aside for one hour.
2 Meanwhile prepare the sauce by placing all the ingredients
in a saucepan. Bring to the boil over a moderate heat
stirring constantly. Lower the heat and simmer for 5 minutes,
stirring occasionally. Remove the pan from the heat and
keep the sauce warm while you grill the meat.
3 Remove the lamb cubes from the bowl and discard the
marinade. Thread on to skewers and grill over charcoal for
15–20 minutes, turning once or twice. Remove the skewers
from the heat and pile on to a serving dish.
4 Pour the sauce into small individual saucers and serve
immediately with the meat. Dip the pieces into the sauce
before eating.

Jamaican bacon – bacon and pineapple roll kebab

These bacon and pineapple rolls make a sizzlingly delicious
kebab, especially when accompanied by an apple and celery
salad or potato-corn salad and frijoles (page 226).

450g (1lb) streaky bacon, rind removed
450g (1lb) tin pineapple cubes
pepper to taste

1 Cut each bacon rasher in half crossways. Roll each
pineapple cube up in one piece of bacon.
2 Spear these 'parcels' on to 6 skewers and season with
freshly ground black pepper. Grill, turning frequently. The
bacon should be nice and crisp.

Pescada espada y melon a la brocheta – fish and melon
kebab

This delightful appetizer from Mexico uses cubes of fish with
cantaloupe melon to create an unusual yet extremely

compatible hors d'oeuvre. It is easy to prepare and cooks within minutes.

Swordfish is not easily available but any firm-fleshed fish will do, e.g. halibut.

750g (1½lb) swordfish, skinned, boned and the flesh cut into 2.5cm (1in) cubes
1 large cantaloupe melon

Marinade
juice of 3 lemons
½ teaspoon salt
2 tablespoons finely chopped spring onions

Garnish
lemon or lime wedges

1 Mix the marinade ingredients together in a large bowl. Add the cubed fish, turn to coat with the marinade, cover and leave for one hour.
2 Halve the melon, remove the skin and seeds and cut the flesh into 2cm (¾in) cubes.
3 Remove the fish cubes from the marinade and thread onto 6 skewers alternating with melon cubes. Cook over charcoal for about 10 minutes turning frequently.
4 Serve immediately with the lemon or lime wedges

Amram – wheat and meat kebab

A simple and interesting kebab from Cilician Armenia (Southern Turkey). The basic ingredients are minced meat and tzavar – better known as burghul or cracked wheat. The wheat is boiled, dried under the sun and then 'cracked' between two large, round stones. Burghul is sold in most continental and health food stores. There are two grades, ask for the 'fine' variety.

225g (½lb) fine burghul
450g (1lb) lamb, minced twice
1 onion, very finely chopped
2 teaspoons cumin
salt and black pepper to taste

Garnish
300ml (½ pint) yoghurt

1 Soak the burghul, in sufficient cold water to cover, for about 10 minutes. Squeeze out any excess water and place in a large bowl. Add the remaining ingredients and knead for several minutes until really smooth. If you keep your hands damp it will make the kneading easier. Divide the mixture into 12 portions and roll each into a ball between dampened palms. Pat each ball around a skewer squeezing it out into a thin sausage shape.
2 Cook over charcoal for about 10 minutes, turning frequently.
3 Serve immediately with yoghurt spooned over them and with a bowl of mixed salad.

Lamb kebabs

Always try to buy the best and most tender cuts you can afford. When cutting the meat use a very sharp knife and cut across the grain, trim off the fat and remove any tendons, tough membranes and ligaments.

Marinate the meat for as long as possible. This not only improves the flavour, but also helps to make the meat more tender. As different meats have different textures, some soak up the juices more quickly than others and so the steeping times vary. The meat with the most tightly knit texture is lamb and you should allow at least 8 hours, but overnight is preferable. If the meat is being marinated in the refrigerator remember to cover it and to remove it from the refrigerator about one hour before cooking.

Lamb is the most popular meat throughout North Africa, the Middle East and Central Asia and consequently almost all the recipes in this book from these regions have lamb as their basis.

When buying lamb it is best to buy a whole leg or shoulder and freeze any unused meat for use at a later date. Lamb has very tender meat with a distinctive flavour. Its meat is very digestible, relatively low in calories with a high protein and low fat content. When buying lamb, its age is an important factor. The younger the animal the more tender the meat and vice-versa. This tender meat should be pink in colour and the cross-section of bone should be moist, porous and red. A layer of fat – which should be firm and white, but not too thick – should cover the leg or shoulder. After a lamb reaches the age of one year it is called a yearling and at this point the animal becomes a breeder.

Leg

Leg of lamb is the last half of the hind saddle. It is the
meatiest part of the animal and the most popular joint from
which kebabs are usually prepared. 'Shish' kebab usually
comes from the fillet end of the leg.

 The whole leg of lamb includes both the shank and the
sirloin and is excellent when roasted. It can be spit-roasted,
whole or boned, rolled and tied.

Chops

Loin lamb chops are the most tender of all chops; they are
usually cut 2.5cm (1in) thick. Blade chops are cut from the
section at the beginning of the shoulder and are large and
meaty but lack the tenderness of rib chops; sirloin chops
and rib chops are small and tasty and have the fat trimmed,
leaving a small circle of meat attached to the bone. Chump
chops are cut from between the leg and the loin.

 Lamb chops can be marinated but are often brushed with a
baste flavoured with herbs and spices and then simply
grilled.

Shoulder

Shoulder of lamb is the front leg portion of the lamb. It is
not as tender as the leg proper for barbecuing purposes.
Your butcher will bone the shoulder and it can then be rolled
and grilled, or cut into small chunks for threading on to
skewers.

 Please note that although the choicest cuts of lamb for
grilling are from leg, loin or shoulder there is no need to
ignore the cheaper cuts – just marinate them longer or mince
them and make some of the minced meat kebabs described
in the book.

 We open our section on lamb with kebabs – chunks of meat
threaded on to skewers. All kebabs should be marinated
well in advance, say 8–12 hours. If not, then they are in
effect simply pieces of grilled meat and nothing more!

Shish kebab – marinated chunks of meat

Young woman to mother:

'Fine, fine, so he is handsome, he is rich, but can he cook a good shish kebab?' Armenian proverb

This is one of the great classics of Middle Eastern cooking. It is originally Caucasian, but now has countless variations and improvisations.

1 It is usually leg of lamb that is used for shish kebab.

2 Remember that the tenderness of the meat will depend upon:

(a) removal of as many tough membranes and ligaments as possible

(b) cutting the meat across the grain

(c) the length of time the meat is left to marinate.

3 Approximately 1kg (2lb) of meat cut into 2.5cm (1in) cubes will provide 6 skewers of meat assuming that about 8 pieces of meat are threaded onto each one.

4 When you have finished preparing the meat you may like to choose one of the following marinades. Each one is sufficient for 1kg (2lb) meat.

5 Mix all the ingredients (unless otherwise directed) for each marinade in a large bowl, add the pieces of meat, stir well until each piece of meat is coated and then cover and refrigerate for several hours. Eight hours is normally sufficient, but overnight is preferable.

(A) Marinade for Shishlig kebab – an Armenian favourite
150ml (¼ pint) oil
150ml (¼ pint) red wine
1 teaspoon allspice
salt and black pepper to taste

(B) Marinade for Souvlaki – a Greek favourite
150ml (¼ pint) oil
Juice 1 lemon
2 onions, chopped and crushed to extract the juice – use a garlic
  press or juice extractor
2 bay leaves
2 teaspoons oregano

pulp of 2 tomatoes
salt and black pepper to taste

(C) Marinade for Sis kebabi – a Turkish version
150ml (¼ pint) oil
2 onions, chopped and crushed to extract the juice – use a garlic
  press or extractor
1 teaspoon cinnamon
salt and black pepper to taste

(D) Marinade for Madznov-shishlig – another Armenian favourite
300ml (½ pint) yoghurt
1 onion, chopped and crushed to extract juice – use garlic press or
  extractor
salt and black pepper to taste

(E) Marinade for Punjabi kobob – a standard Indian marinade
150ml (¼ pint) yoghurt
¼ teaspoon green chilli, chopped very finely
2.5cm (1in) fresh ginger, peeled and finely chopped
½ teaspoon ground coriander
½ teaspoon ground cumin
1 clove garlic, crushed
juice ½ lemon
1 teaspoon salt

(F) Marinade for a Hawaiian speciality
2 tablespoons oil
3 tablespoons vinegar
¼ cup white wine
1 clove garlic, crushed
½ teaspoon dill
½ teaspoon black pepper
1 teaspoon salt
225g (8oz) tin crushed pineapple – fresh pineapple will, of course,
  do equally well!
1 teaspoon rosemary

(G) Marinade for American shish kebab with barbecue sauce
1 teaspoon chilli pepper
1 teaspoon celery salt
2 tablespoons soft brown sugar
2 tablespoons wine vinegar
2 tablespoons Worcestershire sauce
3 tablespoons tomato ketchup

150ml (¼ pint) beef stock
tabasco sauce to taste

(H) Ginger glaze marinade
3 tablespoons stem ginger
1 tablespoon soy sauce
1 tablespoon tomato purée
2 spring onions, white parts cut from the green parts and each
  colour chopped separately
6 tablespoons stock
salt and black pepper to taste

Put all the ingredients, except the chopped green part of the
onions into a small saucepan. Bring to the boil, lower the
heat and simmer for 5 minutes. Cool, pour over the meat,
cover and refrigerate overnight.

   When the kebabs are cooked and ready to be served arrange
the skewers on a dish, heat any remaining marinade in a
small pan and pour it over the meat and garnish with the
chopped green onion.

(I) Marinade for Souvlaki-tou-voskoo – a Cypriot favourite
150ml (¼ pint) red wine
75ml (2½fl oz) vinegar
1 clove garlic, crushed
1 teaspoon salt
¼ teaspoon black pepper
½ teaspoon crushed dried mint
3 sprigs parsley

6 When you are ready to cook the kebabs, thread the pieces
of meat, alternating with pieces of onion if liked, on to
skewers and grill them over charcoal.
7 Turn the skewers occasionally so that the meat cooks
evenly.
8 Cook until brown on the outside, but just a little pink and
juicy in the centre.

Tikka kobob – Indian spiced kebab

This is a classic of the Indian sub-continent. It was introduced
by the invading Muslims from Arabia and Persia and was

'Indianized' in time. Prepare two days in advance.

1kg (2lb) lean lamb, cut into 2.5cm (1in) cubes

Marinade
300ml (½ pint) yoghurt
2 teaspoons garam masala
½ teaspoon ground coriander
½ teaspoon turmeric
2 cloves garlic, crushed
½ teaspoon ground nutmeg
1 teaspoon chilli powder
2 teaspoons ground cumin
grated rind and juice of 2 lemons

1 Mix all the marinade ingredients together in a large bowl.
Add the meat and stir well to ensure that all the cubes are
well coated. Cover and leave to marinate in the refrigerator
for 2 days.
2 Thread the meat cubes on to skewers and grill for 8–10
minutes, turning frequently. The meat should be very
tender so do not overcook.
3 These kebabs are usually eaten with bread – e.g. nan,
lavash or pitta. Garnish with onion rings and lemon wedges.

Mtsawadi – Georgian shish kebab

This Georgian speciality is also sometimes known as 'Tiblisi
Shashlig'. It is traditionally served with pomegranate syrup
which gives this kebab its unique flavour.

1kg (2lb) lean lamb, cut into 2.5cm (1in) cubes
100g (4oz) streaky bacon, rind removed
1 onion
100g (4oz) mushrooms, wiped clean

Marinade
3 cloves garlic, crushed
1 onion, chopped
2 tablespoons chopped parsley
300ml (½ pint) vinegar
1 teaspoon salt
½ teaspoon black pepper

Garnish
1 tablespoon butter, melted
3–4 spring onions, chopped
2 tomatoes, sliced
lemon wedges
pomegranate syrup (page 255)

1 Put all the marinade ingredients into a large bowl and
mix well. Add the cubed meat and stir. Cover and
refrigerate overnight.
2 Cut the bacon into 2.5cm (1in) pieces. Quarter the onion
and separate the various layers.
3 Thread the meat on to skewers alternating with pieces of
bacon and onion and the occasional mushroom. Cook for
10–12 minutes, turning frequently.
4 Slide the kebabs from the skewers onto a large serving
plate and sprinkle them with the melted butter and spring
onions. Garnish with the sliced tomatoes and lemon wedges.
5 Serve with the pomegranate syrup. Either sprinkle a little
over the meat or serve it in very small individual dishes
and dip the chunks of meat in it before eating.

Sosaties – South African kebabs

These South African kebabs are pieces of lamb and fat
threaded onto skewers and grilled. The recipe was brought
to South Africa by the Dutch settlers who had adapted it
from the Indonesian dish saté.

1kg (2lb) shoulder of lamb

Marinade
40g (1½oz) butter
1 large onion, finely chopped
1 tablespoon curry paste or powder
2 teaspoons soft brown sugar
1 teaspoon salt
½ teaspoon black pepper
1 tablespoon fruit chutney
360ml (12fl oz) white wine vinegar
180ml (6fl oz) water
finely grated rind of ½ lemon

1 Trim the lamb of all fat. Cut the meat and fat into small cubes. Thread the meat and fat alternately on to small skewers. Arrange in a large shallow dish and set aside.
2 Melt the butter in a frying pan, add the onion and fry for 8–10 minutes or until soft and golden brown. Add the curry paste or powder, sugar, salt, pepper and chutney and cook, stirring constantly for 2 minutes. Stir in the vinegar, water and lemon rind. Bring to the boil, stirring occasionally. Allow this mixture to cool, then pour evenly over the threaded skewers. Cover and refrigerate for 24 hours, turning the skewers occasionally.
3 When ready to cook remove the skewers from the dish and reserve the marinade. Grill the meat for 8–10 minutes, turning once or twice until cooked.
4 Meanwhile pour the marinade into a small pan, bring to the boil and simmer for about 10 minutes or until reduced by one-third. Strain into a sauceboat.
5 To serve remove the kebabs from the heat, pile on to a platter and serve with the sauce.

Quotban – Moroccan kebab

An authentic Moroccan dish of marinated kebabs. Note the similarity to Indian spicing e.g. the clever use of ginger, hot chillies and cardamom seeds. Quotban may be served in small quantities as a first course or as a main dish with accompanying saffron rice and a yoghurt salad.

1kg (2lb) lean lamb, cut into 2.5cm (1in) cubes
450g (1lb) beef suet, cut into 2.5cm (1in) cubes

Marinade
60ml (2fl oz) lemon juice
120ml (4fl oz) olive oil
½ teaspoon cinnamon
4 cloves garlic, crushed
2 tablespoons chopped parsley
3.5cm (1½in) piece ginger, peeled and chopped
½ teaspoon chilli pepper
½ teaspoon cardamom seeds, crushed

1 teaspoon salt
½ teaspoon black pepper

1 Mix all the marinade ingredients together in a large bowl.
Add the lamb cubes and stir until all are well coated. Leave
to marinate at room temperature for about 4 hours, turning
occasionally.
2 Thread the cubes on to skewers evenly, interspersed with
pieces of suet.
3 Grill for 10–12 minutes or until the lamb is tender and
the suet is crisp, turning occasionally. Serve immediately.

Peleponnesiako souvlaki – lamb marinated in cumin and
nuts. A delicious kebab, which is served on a bed of noodles.

1kg (2lb) lean lamb, cut into 2.5cm (1in) cubes
450g (1lb) noodles
75g (3oz) butter, cut into small pieces

Baste
2 tablespoons olive oil
2 tablespoons red wine vinegar
1 tablespoon lemon juice
1 teaspoon crushed cumin seeds or ground cumin
¼ teaspoon black pepper
1½ teaspoons salt
3 tablespoons pine nuts, crushed

1 Thread the lamb cubes onto skewers and set aside.
2 In a small bowl mix together the oil, vinegar, lemon juice,
cumin seeds, pepper, half the salt and half the nuts. Using
a pastry brush, brush the lamb cubes with half of this oil
mixture. Grill the kebabs, turning and brushing frequently
with the remaining oil mixture for 10–12 minutes or until
the lamb is cooked through and tender.
4 Meanwhile half fill a large saucepan with water, add the
remaining salt and bring to the boil. Reduce heat to
moderate, add the noodles and, stirring once or twice with a
fork, cook them for 6–8 minutes or until they are *al dente*
i.e. just tender. Remove pan from the heat and drain noodles
into a colander. Transfer to a large serving platter. Add the

butter and, using two large spoons, toss the noodles until the butter has melted and they are thoroughly coated. Set aside and keep warm.

5 When the kebabs are cooked, slide the lamb cubes on to the noodles, sprinkle remaining nuts over the top and serve immediately.

Kebab halabi – Aleppo-style kebab

'May Allah be praised, our work is done and our souls are at peace. . . .' Arab expression

This kebab comes from Aleppo in Syria, one of the great centres of Middle Eastern cooking and especially famed for its cheeses, sweets and kebabs. The cuisine of Aleppo is interesting for it has evolved through the ages absorbing Assyrian, Turkish, Armenian, Crusader and Arab influences into what today is regarded as the 'backbone' of the Arab kitchen.

1kg (2lb) lean lamb, cut into 2.5cm (1in) cubes
2 tablespoons olive oil
juice of 1 onion (obtained by crushing the onion in a garlic press or mincer)
3 pitta bread
50g (2oz) butter or ghee, melted
3 large tomatoes
½ teaspoon salt
450ml (¾ pint) yoghurt
6 spring onions, finely chopped
1 tablespoon parsley, finely chopped

1 Put the lamb cubes into a large bowl, add the oil and onion juice, mix well and leave to marinate at room temperature for 2 hours.

2 When you have prepared the fire and are ready to cook the kebabs first warm the pittas for a minute or two over the fire. Cut the bread into 1cm (½in) wide strips and place on a large platter. Pour the melted butter or ghee over the bread, mix well, arrange the places neatly and set aside.

3 Thread the pieces of meat on to skewers and grill over

charcoal for 10–12 minutes or until tender, turning
occasionally.
4 Meanwhile peel and chop the tomatoes. Put into a small
pan, season with the salt and cook gently for about 3
minutes.
5 When the kebabs are cooked first spoon the tomatoes over
the bread and then slide the kebabs off the skewers onto
the tomatoes. Pour the yoghurt over the meat, sprinkle with
the chopped onions and parsley and serve immediately.

Boti kebabs – lamb in spicy yoghurt mixture

This Indian dish, popular throughout Northern India and
Hyderabad is usually eaten with *chapattis* (page 206), but
it may also be served with rice or *non* (page 205).

1kg (2lb) lean lamb, cut into 2.5cm (1in) cubes

Marinade
150ml (5fl oz) yoghurt
1 tablespoon ground coriander
1 teaspoon turmeric
1 teaspoon chilli pepper
1 teaspoon salt
2 cloves garlic, crushed
2.5cm (1in) piece ginger, peeled and grated or finely chopped

Garnish
1 tablespoon finely chopped coriander leaves, optional
lemon wedges

1 Mix all the marinade ingredients together in a large bowl.
Add the lamb cubes and toss until well coated. Cover and
refrigerate for at least 6 hours, but preferably overnight.
2 Thread the cubes on to skewers and grill over charcoal for
10–12 minutes, turning frequently.
3 Place on a serving dish, sprinkle with the coriander and
garnish with lemon wedges

Seekh kabob kari – kebab in curry sauce

This recipe from Northern India/Pakistan is best served with rice pilav. The meat is first grilled over charcoal then it is either added to the curry sauce or, as I prefer, it is laid on a bed of rice and the sauce is then poured over the top.

1kg (2lb) lamb or beef steaks, cut into 4cm (1½in) cubes

Marinade
1 teaspoon ground cumin
1 teaspoon garam masala
1 teaspoon ground coriander
½ teaspoon turmeric
½ teaspoon ground ginger
2 cloves garlic, crushed
3–4 tablespoons oil
1 teaspoon salt
¼ teaspoon grated nutmeg
2 tablespoons lemon juice

Curry sauce
4 tablespoons melted butter or ghee
1 onion, finely chopped
2 cloves garlic, crushed
5cm (2in) cinnamon stick
2 cardamom pods, bruised
2 cloves
1 teaspoon chilli pepper
1 teaspoon garam masala
2 tablespoons finely chopped parsley
90ml (3fl oz) water

1 Mix all the marinade ingredients together in a large bowl. Add the meat and mix thoroughly until it is well coated. Cover and refrigerate overnight.
2 Thread the meat on to skewers and grill over charcoal for 15–20 minutes, turning frequently.
3 Meanwhile prepare the sauce by heating the ghee or butter in a pan and then adding the onion and garlic and frying until soft. Add the remaining ingredients, stir thoroughly and then simmer until the sauce thickens.
4 When the kebabs are cooked either slide the meat off the skewers into the sauce or else lay them on rice and pour the sauce over the top.

Kabaub afghani – Afghan-style kebab

Afghan food is a cross between Iranian and Indian as these charming kebabs illustrate.

The yoghurt marinade gives the kebab an extra tenderness as well as flavour. The ideal way to eat this kebab is to fill the pocket of a warm pitta bread with it or to wrap the kebab in thin lavash bread.

1kg (2lb) lean lamb, cut into 2.5cm (1in) cubes

Marinade
300ml (½ pint) yoghurt
2 cloves garlic, crushed
1 teaspoon salt
½ teaspoon black pepper

To serve
6 pitta bread
3 large tomatoes, thinly sliced
1 large onion, thinly sliced
1 lemon
Fresh sprigs tarragon or coriander

1 Mix the marinade ingredients together in a large bowl. Add the meat cubes, stir to coat well, cover and refrigerate for at least 6 hours.
2 Thread meat on to skewers and cook over charcoal for 10–12 minutes, turning and basting frequently with any remaining marinade.
3 Meanwhile warm the pittas on the grill and when they blow up like a balloon remove and slit through the middle to form a pocket. Place some tomato and onion slices in each pocket and then push the meat off the skewers and into the pittas. Squeeze a little lemon juice over each filling. Garnish with the tarragon or coriander and serve immediately.

Karski shashlig – chunks of lamb and kidney on skewers

It was during the first Russo-Turkish wars of the nineteenth century that Russian soldiers were first introduced to this dish in the city of Kars (Eastern Turkey). It is now highly popular throughout the USSR.

These kebabs are usually served on small flaming swords with a great deal of pomp and circumstance in the emigré Russian restaurants of Paris and New York.

1kg (2lb) lean lamb cut into 12 large pieces
9 sheep's kidneys, halved

Marinade
1 onion, chopped
2 tablespoons chopped parsley
3 tablespoons vinegar or lemon juice
1 teaspoon salt
½ teaspoon black pepper

Garnish
Lemon wedges

1 Mix the marinade ingredients together in a large bowl. Add the lamb pieces and halved kidneys and mix well. Cover and refrigerate for at least 8 hours or overnight.
2 Thread 2 pieces meat on to each skewer with each piece sandwiched between kidney halves (i.e. 2 pieces of meat and 3 kidney halves on each skewer).
3 Cook for 20–30 minutes, turning and basting frequently with any remaining marinade. Serve with plain rice and the lemon wedges.

Lamb chops

Whatever type of chops you are using, e.g. blade, rib, loin, arm etc., trim off as much of the fat as possible.

Allow about 12–15 minutes cooking time and serve with salads, rice and/or other accompaniments.

Lamb chops à l'americaine – American-style lamb chops

6 large lamb chops, about 2.5cm (1in) thick

Dressing
3 tablespoons grated parmesan or cheddar cheese
2 tablespoons butter or mayonnaise

½ teaspoon salt
¼ teaspoon black pepper
½ teaspoon paprika

1 Arrange the chops on the grill and cook over charcoal for about 12–15 minutes, turning occasionally.
2 Mix the dressing ingredients together in a small bowl. Spread it over the chops and grill for a further 2 minutes. Remove from the fire and serve with salads and pickles of your choice.

Cotelettes d'agneau bar-man – Bar-man lamb chops

This is what the French think the English (and Americans) eat for their business lunches!

6 large lamb chops, trimmed of fat
3 large tomatoes, halved
12 button mushrooms, wiped clean
6 rashers bacon

Garnishes
watercress, radishes, cucumber slices and grated carrots

1 Arrange the chops on the grill and cook over charcoal for 12–15 minutes, turning occasionally. Meanwhile thread the tomatoes and mushrooms onto skewers and grill until cooked. About 5 minutes before the chops are cooked lay the bacon rashers on the grill and cook.
2 Arrange the chops on a large platter and top each one with a bacon rasher. Slide the grilled vegetables onto the platter and decorate with the various garnishes.

Ararat khorovu – lamb chops with tomatoes

A famed Armenian kebab usually served on small swords with great gusto.

12 lamb chops
6 tomatoes
12 mushrooms, wiped clean
2 green peppers, each cut into 6 pieces
24 pieces onion

Marinade
150ml (¼ pint) oil
150ml (¼ pint) red wine
1 clove garlic, crushed
1 teaspoon salt
½ teaspoon black pepper
1 teaspoon allspice

1 Mix all the marinade ingredients together in a large bowl.
Add the chops and turn until well coated. Cover and
refrigerate overnight.
2 If you have 6 long skewers then thread 2 chops onto each
one alternating with 1 tomato, 2 mushrooms, 2 pieces green
pepper and 4 pieces onion. Otherwise cook the chops on the
grill, thread the vegetables onto 2 skewers and then
apportion chops and vegetables afterwards.

As with Karski Shashlig (page 52) this kebab is best served
on swords set alight with a piece of cotton-wool near the
handle. In this way it is an extremely impressive-looking
dish.

Lelakha kobob – Punjabi lamb chops kebab

This marinade of yoghurt and spices gives the chops a strong
flavour that is best appreciated with a saffron rice pilav or
a pilav with pineapple and cashew nuts.

These kebabs are traditionally cooked in a tandoori clay
oven over charcoal, but they taste just as good cooked in the
normal way over charcoal.

12 lamb chops
6 tomatoes

Marinade
1 large onion, chopped
2 tablespoons ground coriander
1 teaspoon salt
1½ teaspoons cumin
½ teaspoon black pepper
½ teaspoon ground ginger
½ teaspoon cinnamon
½ teaspoon ground cardamom

½ teaspoon poppy seeds
2 tablespoons melted butter or ghee
450ml (¾ pint) yoghurt
juice 1 large lemon

1 Place the marinade ingredients in a liquidizer and blend
to a smooth paste.
2 Arrange the chops in a shallow dish and pour the marinade
evenly over them. Turn the chops so that they are well
coated, cover and refrigerate overnight.
3 Thread 2 chops onto each skewer together with 1 tomato.
Cook over charcoal, turning several times until the chops
are cooked through. Serve with a rice pilav of your choice.

Leg of lamb

Leg of lamb should be spit-roasted to retain its juices.

Ask your butcher to cut about 5–7.5cm (2in–3in) of the bone
off the small end of the leg, leaving the meat to form a flap
which can then be folded over the remaining bone and held
in place by the spit.

Allow approximately 30 minutes per 450g (1lb).

Incisions are often made in the flesh; garlic, peppercorns
and herbs and spices are inserted.

Gigot d'agneau roti – roast leg of lamb

This standard Franco-English recipe is self-explanatory.
Serve it with mint sauce and vegetables of your choice.

1½–2kg (3–4lb) leg of lamb
3 cloves garlic, halved lengthways
1 teaspoon salt
½ teaspoon oregano
3–4 tablespoons melted butter
juice of 1 lemon

1 Make six incisions in the lamb and insert the pieces of
garlic. Mix the salt and oregano together and rub all over
the meat.
2 Position the meat on a spit and cook over charcoal for

about 2 hours or until cooked through. Baste the joint
frequently with a mixture of the butter and lemon juice.

Kouzou karni – stuffed roast leg of lamb

A Syrian version of roast leg of lamb.

1½–2kg (3–4lb) leg of lamb – ask your butcher to bone it, leaving
 a pocket
50g (2oz) butter, melted

Stuffing
50g (2oz) dried figs, chopped
100g (4oz) prunes, stoned and chopped
100g (4oz) raisins
½ teaspoon thyme
½ teaspoon sage

1 Mix all the stuffing ingredients together and fill the pocket
in the meat. Sew or tie up the end of the joint and secure on
a spit.
2 Cook over charcoal for about 2 hours or until cooked
through, turning and basting frequently with the melted
butter

Variation – a Yemeni version
1½–2kg (3–4lb) leg of lamb – ask your butcher to bone it leaving
 a pocket
2 tablespoons oil
1 teaspoon salt
½ teaspoon black pepper
½ teaspoon thyme
½ teaspoon rosemary
2 tablespoons chopped fresh mint OR 2 teaspoons dried mint
2 bay leaves
100g (4oz) dates, stoned and chopped

1 In a small bowl mix together the oil, salt and pepper. Brush
the inside and outside of the meat with this mixture.
2 In another small bowl mix together the thyme, rosemary
and mint. Rub these herbs into the meat both inside and
out.
3 Place the bay leaves and the chopped dates in the pocket

of the meat and sew or tie up the opening. Secure the leg
on the spit.
4 Cook over charcoal for about 2 hours or until cooked
through, turning and basting frequently with a little oil.

Collier's roast – an old English recipe

Colliers were charcoal burners and were apparently famed
as poachers in medieval England. When they had an extra
lamb or two, in order to avoid discovery, they salted the legs
of the lambs in brine and when the rest of the lamb was
eaten they would remove a leg from the brine, wash it
thoroughly and grill it over a fire.

Meat preserved in this way will be reddish in colour and
naturally have a slightly salty flavour.

Khorovadze – the whole roast lamb

'She has no dowry sir, but her cooking is divine!' – Arab expression

This is whole roast lamb on a spit. Whole roast lamb is a
festive, ceremonial repast in the Middle East prepared for
parties, festivals and family gatherings.

The Muslims celebrate their holy day of Eid-el-Kurban by
sacrificing a whole lamb and cooking it with the eyes
blackened (or removed), a piece of confectionery placed in the
mouth and its head turned towards Mecca. It is then roasted
on a spit and the meat distributed to the poor.

In Armenia the lamb is first blessed by a priest, then
slaughtered ceremonially, with people dipping a finger in
the blood. Then the animal is cleaned and roasted and, as
with the Muslim tradition, it is eaten by host, guests and
passers-by.

This then could be the ideal exotic dinner. A whole lamb is
enough for 30 people. Give your butcher 2–3 days' notice if
you wish to order one.

15kg (30–35lb) lamb, rinsed thoroughly inside and out and wiped
dry.

Rub, inside and out with salt and black pepper, then sprinkle with onion juice (made by crushing an onion in a garlic press or mincer). In Morocco they make a very tasty paste using:

2 tablespoons ground coriander
5 cloves garlic, crushed
2 teaspoons cumin
1 tablespoon paprika
100g (4oz) softened butter
salt and pepper to taste

1 Beat these ingredients together to form a smooth paste and then rub into the inside and outside of the lamb.
2 Push a wooden or metal rod right through the lamb from the breast to the hindquarters. Truss the legs together. The long spit should rest on supports rising approximately 30–45cm (1ft–1ft 6in) from the ground. The spit usually has a handle to ease the turning of the lamb.
3 Baste frequently while it is cooking and allow at least 4–4½ hours for cooking.

Minced meat

Kofta kebab is the general name given, throughout the Middle East to minced meat kebabs, but each region naturally has its own favourite seasonings.

Basic recipe

1kg (2lb) lamb (or beef or a mixture of both), minced twice
2 onions, very finely chopped
1 large or 2 small eggs
Salt and pepper to taste

1 Put all the ingredients into a large bowl and knead together until very smooth.
2 Keeping your hands damp take an egg-sized lump and mould it firmly around a skewer squeezing the meat out gently until the kebab is thin and sausage-shaped. If possible

use flat skewers so that the meat will not slip when the skewers are turned.

3 Cook on a well oiled grill for about 10 minutes, turning frequently.

The following is a very tasty Moroccan variation:

1kg (2lb) lamb, minced
2 onions, finely chopped
4 tablespoons chopped parsley
2 teaspoons dried marjoram or oregano
1 teaspoon cumin
½ teaspoon harissa (see page 254)
Salt and pepper to taste

Prepare and cook as described above.

Soong kebab – kofta with mushrooms

Ingredients for basic recipe for kofta kebab and 48 button mushrooms.

1 Prepare as for kofta kebab.

2 Keeping your hands damp divide the meat mixture into 36 small balls.

3 Thread the balls and mushrooms alternately onto skewers. Allow 3 meatballs and 4 mushrooms per skewer. Take care with the mushrooms as they may split when pierced. They are easier to handle if you soak them in warm water for 10 minutes first.

4 Cook as for kofta kebab.

Yerevan kebab – a mixture of soong and shish kebab

Allow one skewer of soong kebab and one skewer of shish kebab per person. Therefore if cooking for 6 prepare half the quantity of the basic shish kebab recipe and half the quantity of the soong recipe.

Serve with a skewer of tomato quarters alternating with slices of green pepper and onion – allow one skewer per person.

Lule kebab – Armenian kofta kebab

1kg (2lb) minced lamb
2 onions, very finely chopped
2 tablespoons finely chopped parsley
Salt and black pepper to taste

Vegetables
12 tomatoes
1 large onion, finely chopped
4 tablespoons finely chopped parsley

1 Put the minced meat, onion, parsley and seasonings into
a large bowl and, with damp hands, knead until the mixture
is well blended and smooth. Take an egg-sized lump, pass a
skewer through it and squeeze the meat out gently until
the kebab is thin and sausage-shaped.
2 Cook on a well oiled grill, turning frequently for about 10
minutes.
3 At the same time thread the tomatoes on to skewers and
cook them over the fire.
4 When the kebabs are cooked and ready to serve, remove
the tomatoes from the fire to a large plate and skin them.
Chop the flesh, place it in a bowl and mix in the onion and
parsley.
5 Whether serving the kebabs from a central platter or on
individual dishes use the tomato mixture as a base and
place the kebabs on top.

Urfa kebab – aubergine and meatball kebab

This is a kebab from the city of Urfa in Southern Turkey.

Ingredients as for kofta kebab and
4 aubergines

1 Divide the meat mixture into 36 balls.
2 Trim the aubergine and then cut into 1cm (½in) thick
rings (do not cut them any thicker or they will not be tender
by the time the meat has cooked). Thread the meatballs and
aubergine slices alternately on to skewers.
3 Cook as for kofta kebab, turning frequently. Serve with

lavash bread (page 207) and a garnish of onion rings and fresh tomato slices.

Khash-khash – minced meat kebab on a bed of bread and tomatoes. This Armenian kebab is similar to lule kebab, but features the addition of bread and garlic.

Ingredients for lule kebab and
1 teaspoon chilli pepper
1 clove garlic, finely chopped
6 pitta bread

1 Follow the instructions for lule kebab adding the chilli pepper to the meat mixture.
2 Prepare and cook the kebabs and tomatoes over the charcoal. When nearly cooked warm the pitta over the fire and then place on a large plate. Put the cooked kebabs on top of them. The fat from the kebabs will soften and flavour the bread. Keep warm while you prepare the vegetables.
3 Skin the tomatoes, chop the flesh and place it in a bowl. Add the chopped onion, parsley and the garlic and mix well.
4 Whether serving the kebabs on a central dish or on individual plates use the tomato mixture as a base, place the kebabs on top, cut each bread into 4 pieces and arrange them on top of the kebabs. Serve immediately.

Madzounov kebab – meat balls with yoghurt and topped with omelette. This is a well-known Armenian kebab which is also popular in Southern Turkey and Northern Syria.

1kg (2lb) lamb, minced twice
2 onions, very finely chopped
1 egg
2 tablespoons finely chopped parsley
salt and pepper to taste
1 clove garlic, crushed
450ml (¾ pint) yoghurt
6 pitta bread
1 tablespoon butter
6 eggs

salt and pepper to taste
½ teaspoon chilli pepper

1 Put the meat, onion, egg, parsley, salt and pepper into a
large bowl and knead until well blended and smooth.
Keeping your hands damp form the mixture into balls about
2.5cm (1in) in diameter. Thread the balls onto skewers and
cook over charcoal for about 10 minutes or until cooked
through, turning frequently.
2 Meanwhile stir the garlic into the yoghurt.
3 Cut 3 pittas into 8 segments each and arrange them over
the bottom of a large platter.
4 Melt the butter in a large frying pan. Crack the eggs into
a bowl and beat in salt and pepper to taste. Pour into the
frying pan and cook over a gentle heat.
5 When the meat and omelette are ready slide the meatballs
on to the bread. Pour the yoghurt over the meat and bread
and sprinkle with the chilli pepper. Slide the whole omelette
on top of the yoghurt.
6 Cut the remaining 3 pittas into 8 segments each and
arrange them around the edge of the platter. Serve
immediately.

Seekh kebab – Indian minced meat kebab

This is an Indian version of the kofta kebab. Very often the
skewers used on the sub-continent are as thick as a pencil
so that the meat can be spread out thinly and thus cooked
quickly.

1kg (2lb) lean lamb, minced
2 onions, roughly chopped
4 tablespoons fresh breadcrumbs
2 tablespoons chopped fresh coriander
1 teaspoon salt
2 teaspoons garam masala
2 tablespoons lemon juice OR mango juice

Baste
4 tablespoons yoghurt, optional

Garnish
shredded lettuce
cucumber slices

1 Put the meat, onions, breadcrumbs, coriander, salt and
garam masala in a large bowl and knead to mix. Pass
through a mincer. Return to the bowl and continue kneading
until it is smooth and dough-like. Add the lemon or mango
juice and knead in thoroughly. With damp hands form the
mixture into balls about 5cm (2in) in diameter.
2 Still keeping your hands damp pass a skewer through each
ball and gently squeeze the meat out until it forms a thin
sausage shape.
3 Cook over charcoal for 6–8 minutes or until cooked
through, turning and basting frequently with the yoghurt
if using it.
5 Slide the kebabs on to a bed of shredded lettuce and sliced
cucumber and serve with fresh mint chutney (page 252).

For a variation to the flavour of this kebab add:
2.5cm (1in) piece fresh ginger, peeled and finely chopped
2 teaspoons cumin
½ teaspoon chilli pepper
2 green chillies, finely chopped

These ingredients are added to seekh kebabs, more especially
in Northern India where the Moghuls asserted their
influence and both enriched and elaborated the then rather
simple Indian cusine.

Kebab-e-koubideh – Persian minced meat kebab

This, and its companion *Chelo kabab* (page 81) are the two
great achievements of Persian cooking. When we consider
the fact that the people of the Persian-speaking lands were
some of the very first to adopt and eat kebabs one is very
struck by the poor and meagre use of a great culinary
tradition.
 Persian cooking, which is perhaps the poorest of all the
Middle Eastern cuisines when it comes to the use of
vegetables, variety of ingredients and the imaginative use of

spices and materials generally, has, however, with *kebab-e-koubideh* and *chelo kebab* created two unique dishes.

1kg (2lb) minced lamb (beef can also be used)
1 large onion, finely chopped
1 teaspoon salt

To serve
sumac (see page 255)
butter
6 egg yolks

1 Place the meat, onion and salt in a large bowl. With damp hands knead until well blended and smooth. Divide the mixture into egg-sized lumps and, with damp hands, pat each lump around a skewer (flat ones are preferable) and squeeze the meat out firmly until it is thin and sausage-shaped.
2 Cook over a charcoal fire, turning frequently so that the meat is cooked through.
3 To serve, slide two kebabs from the skewers on to each plate. Cover the plates with chelo rice (page 195) or a plain rice pilav and sprinkle with sumac. Top each mound of rice with a knob of butter and an egg yolk.
4 To eat stir the rice so that the egg, butter and sumac are all mixed together. This dish is usually eaten with a spoon rather than a fork. Some Iranians like to eat rings of raw onion and a grilled tomato with this dish.

Kebab Massalam – spicy minced meat kebab

These spicy kebabs are similar to lule kebabs (page 61). Serve them with Indian or Arab bread, a cucumber and tomato salad and yoghurt.

1kg (2lb) minced lamb or beef
3 cloves garlic, crushed
3.5cm (1½in) piece fresh ginger, peeled and finely chopped
2 green chillies, finely chopped
1 large onion, finely chopped
3 tablespoons chopped coriander leaves
4 tablespoons yoghurt
1 teaspoon turmeric

2 tablespoons lemon juice
1½ teaspoons salt
25g (1oz) fresh breadcrumbs
25g (1oz) butter or ghee, melted

To serve
lemon wedges

1 Place all the ingredients except the butter in a large bowl.
Knead until thoroughly mixed and smooth. Cover and set
aside at room temperature for 30 minutes.
2 With damp hands remove small pieces of the mixture and
shape them into 'cigar shapes' around the skewers, two to
a skewer.
3 Lay the skewers on a greased grill and brush them all over
with some of the butter. Cook over charcoal for about 8–10
minutes, turning and basting frequently with the remaining
butter.
4 Place on a serving dish and garnish with the lemon
wedges.

Cevapcici – Yugoslav minced meatball kebab

These skewered lamb and beef balls are a Yugoslavian
favourite. They can be served on the skewers or removed
just before serving.
  Serve with small hot peppers, a cooked vegetable dish and
plain boiled rice.

1 tablespoon butter
2 onions, finely chopped
2 cloves garlic, finely chopped
450g (1lb) minced lamb
450g (1lb) minced beef
50g (2oz) fresh breadcrumbs
1 egg white, lightly beaten
1 teaspoon dried basil
1½ teaspoons salt
1 tablespoon paprika
½ teaspoon chilli pepper

1 Melt the butter in a frying pan, add half the onion and the garlic and fry gently for about 10 minutes, stirring occasionally. Remove from the heat and spoon the contents of the pan into a large bowl. Add all the remaining ingredients and mix with a fork. Knead until smooth and well blended.

2 Damp your hands and divide the mixture into walnut-sized balls. Arrange them on a large plate, cover with greaseproof paper and refrigerate for at least one hour.

3 Thread the meatballs on to skewers and grill for about 8–10 minutes or until the meat is cooked through, turning occasionally.

4 Arrange the skewers on a large platter, sprinkle with the remaining onion and serve immediately.

Saté kambing madura – Indonesian goat's meat kebab

This Indonesian kebab actually uses goat's meat, but as it is not always readily available, lamb is a perfectly good substitute.

There is more information on *saté* in the chapter on beef as it is more of a beef speciality.

700g (1½lb) goat or lamb meat, minced twice
2 large onions, finely chopped
3 cloves garlic, finely chopped
4 large red chillies, seeded and finely chopped
1 tablespoon ground coriander
1 teaspoon cumin
¼ teaspoon kentjur (see Glossary, page 254). This is optional as it is quite difficult to find.
1 tablespoon brown sugar
175g (6oz) desiccated coconut
¼ teaspoon *terasi* (see Glossary, page 255)
1 tablespoon lemon juice
4 kemiri nuts, chopped (or Brazil nuts or walnuts)

1 Mix all the ingredients together in a large bowl and knead thoroughly. Leave to stand at room temperature for 30–45 minutes. With damp hands divide the mixture into walnut-

sized balls. Thread on to skewers and grill over charcoal for
8–10 minutes, turning occasionally until the meat is cooked
through.
2 Serve the kebabs with *kuah saté*, a peanut sauce (see page
249).

Shigadi Me Lemany – Liver with lime

'The Turki is a burly man and a voracious eater, and there is always
a crowd in that part of the bazaar where food is sold. One group
of men, squatting on their heels, surround the cook, who sells
snippets of meat and kidney speared on an iron skewer and grilled
over a portable charcoal fire. This grilled meat is very tasty, though
generally tough.' – *Gobi Desert* by Mildred Cable and Francesca
French, Hurst and Blackett Ltd, London, 1942.

A Greek kebab that is often served as a starter and is
particularly good with a fresh salad, olives and a glass of
ouzo. It also makes an excellent entrée with a rice pilav.

1kg (2lb) lamb's liver, cut into 5cm (2in) cubes
juice 2 limes
½ teaspoon salt
1 tablespoon chopped fresh oregano OR 2 teaspoons dried oregano

Garnish
6 large tomatoes, thickly sliced
2 onions, thickly sliced

1 Put the liver cubes in a large bowl and sprinkle with the
lime juice, salt and oregano. Turn so that the meat is well
coated and set aside at room temperature for about 30
minutes.
2 Thread the meat on to skewers and cook over charcoal for
8–10 minutes, turning occasionally.
3 While they are cooking place the tomato and onion slices,
brushed with oil and seasoned with a little salt and oregano
around the edge of the grill to cook.
4 Serve the liver on a bed of rice and garnish with the tomato
and onion slices.

Bomidorov liart – Liver with tomato

An Armenian way of grilling liver.

1kg (2lb) lamb's liver, cut into 3.5cm (1½in) cubes
2 tablespoons tomato purée
1 clove garlic, crushed
juice 2 lemons
1 teaspoon chilli pepper
1 teaspoon salt
1 teaspoon cumin

1 Mix all the ingredients together in a large bowl making sure that all the pieces of liver are well coated. Leave to stand at room temperature for 30 minutes.
2 Thread the meat on to skewers and cook over charcoal for 8–10 minutes.
3 Serve with a fresh salad.

Kouah – North African liver kebab

This recipe for lamb's liver kebabs from Morocco, with its cumin-scented meat and hot spicy onions conjures up the essence of warm Arabian nights and succulent North African cooking.

Serve with a plain rice pilav and a cool, refreshing salad.

1kg (2lb) lamb's liver, cut into 5cm (2in) cubes
1 tablespoon lemon juice
1 teaspoon salt
½ teaspoon black pepper
60ml (2fl oz) plus 2 tablespoons olive oil
4 tablespoons cumin seeds
3 medium onions, thinly sliced
1 tablespoon harissa sauce (page 254)

1 Place the liver cubes in a shallow dish, sprinkle with the lemon juice and set aside for 10 minutes. Pat dry with kitchen paper and then rub the salt and pepper into the meat. Brush the cubes with the 2 tablespoons oil. Spread the cumin seeds on a plate and roll the meat cubes in them, one by one.

2 Thread the cubes onto skewers, roll them in the cumin seeds again and place on the grill. Cook for 8–10 minutes, turning occasionally until tender.

3 Meanwhile heat the remaining oil in a frying pan, add the onions and fry, stirring occasionally, until soft but not brown. Stir in the harissa and mix well, cooking for a further minute.

4 Transfer the onions to a large serving dish and place the kebabs on top. Serve immediately.

Brochettes de rognons et foie de mouton – kidney and liver kebab

These kidney and liver brochettes are a contribution from France. They are easy and inexpensive and make an excellent lunch or supper dish.

450g (1lb) lamb's liver, cut into 2.5cm (1in) cubes
450g (1lb) veal kidneys, cubed

Marinade
4 tablespoons olive oil
6 tablespoons dry red wine
1 teaspoon dried thyme
½ teaspoon salt
¼ teaspoon black pepper

1 Mix the marinade ingredients together in a large bowl, add the meat cubes and stir until well coated. Leave to stand at room temperature for at least 4 hours.

2 Thread the liver and kidney cubes alternately onto skewers. Cook over charcoal for about 10 minutes, turning regularly and basting with any remaining marinade.

Kokoretsi tis souvlas – sweetbread, liver and kidney kebab

Another classic Middle Eastern kebab highly appreciated by Greeks, Turks and Armenians. The recipe below is from Greece.

Sausage casings can be bought from most butchers – advance notice will probably be necessary.

Although usually served as an appetizer, Turks and Armenians prefer it as a main dish with salads and a bowl of yoghurt.

225g (8oz) sweetbreads
juice of 2 lemons
450g (1lb) lamb's liver
2 lamb's hearts
2 lamb's kidneys, halved
½ teaspoon

Marinade
1 onion, thinly sliced
juice 1 large lemon
120ml (4fl oz) oil
1 teaspoon oregano
3 tablespoons finely chopped parsley
1 teaspoon salt
½ teaspoon black pepper

sausage casings

1 Ask your butcher for veal or lamb sweetbreads which should be white and tender. Soak the sweetbreads in cold water for 20–25 minutes. Drain, place in a saucepan, cover with cold water and simmer for 2 minutes, then drain. Remove the tubes which connect the pairs of sweetbreads, and the outer membranes. Then pat dry and reserve.
2 Put the liver, heart and kidneys into a bowl and add cold water to cover by 5cm (2in). Add the remaining lemon juice and leave to soak for 30 minutes. Drain.
3 Trim any large tubes from the liver and heart and remove the fatty core from the kidneys. Cut all the meats into 3.5cm (1½in) pieces and place in a large bowl.
4 Mix the marinade ingredients together in a small bowl and pour over the meat. Toss well, cover and refrigerate for 2–3 hours.
5 Meanwhile soak the sausage casings in a bowl of cold water.
6 Remove the meat from the refrigerator and thread the various kinds of meat alternately onto skewers.
7 Drain the sausage casings and then open one end of one

and slide it over the meat on the skewer. Trim off any skin
not used. Repeat until you have enclosed all the kebabs.
8 Grill over charcoal for 15–20 minutes, turning and
brushing frequently with the remaining marinade.
9 Serve with lemon wedges as an appetizer or as a main dish
with salads, pickles, yoghurt and rice.

'He burnest part thereof in the fire; with part thereof he eateth
flesh; he roasteth roast, and is satisfied:' – *Isaiah 44, 16*

Beef and veal kebabs

Beef

'The old idea of cooking meat was to employ a naked flame. Ovens of any kind were at first resented, and one must admit that a joint, so long as it is sufficiently large, is undoubtably far superior when roasted in front of a fire on a jack. Anyone who really appreciates cooked meat must surely prefer a steak or chop grilled, to anything cooked in an oven or fried.' – *English Countryside and Gardens*, by Montague G. Allwood, 2 vols, published by Wivelsfield Green, London, 1945

Beef comes from castrated bullocks and young heifers which have never calved. The best beef comes from young animals and it is then matured or 'hung', usually for 10–12 days to tenderize the meat. The best meat should have a bright red colour and be firm and elastic to the touch. It should be marbled with small streaks of white and lightly yellowish fat.

Avoid buying beef that has a very dark colour and appears dry – the meat probably comes from an old animal.

The recipes included in this chapter reflect the countries and regions where beef is more often used than other meats. There is little beef in Africa, the Middle East and Asia in general. Therefore we have to turn to Europe, America and the Far East to find exciting beef barbecues. A point to note is that beef has a much more definite taste and texture than lamb and should be cooked quite differently, therefore it is not advisable to interchange the meats.

In your friendly butcher's shop you will find all the following cuts suitable for grilling:

Fillet steak – taken from the undercut of sirloin, expensive but tender. A large whole fillet can weigh up to 1.25–1.5kg (2½–3lb) and makes an excellent roast. More usually, it is cut into 175–225g (6–8oz) pieces and grilled.

T-bone – taken from porterhouse steak. T-bones are very tender and excellent when barbecued.

Sirloin – this joint usually weighs about 2kg (4lb). Can be boned and rolled. When served as a roast it is treated exactly as rib of beef.

Rib steak – not as tender as sirloin and tends to have much more fat, but nevertheless very tasty. Rib steaks come from the rib section – the front part of the fore quarter. Ribs are excellent when grilled.

Porterhouse – the most popular steak cut, particularly in North America. Very tender with a marvellous flavour.

Chuck steak – comes from the shoulder of beef and should be reasonably priced. Unfortunately not very tender and so I suggest you marinate it in oil and spices before grilling. Has an excellent flavour and very little fat.

Most of the recipes in this collection can be prepared with any of the above beef cuts. The final choice is yours.

Veal

When buying veal make sure that the grain is fine and the colour a light pink. Veal does not keep well. I suggest that you buy it as close to your barbecue date as possible.

For barbecues in general and kebabs in particular the most suitable cuts are best and neck cutlets, fillet loin, loin chops and shoulder.

Incidentally, calf's liver is very tender and tasty when teamed with onion and bacon.

Grilled steaks

A simple recipe which makes an excellent grill. Any meat
cut of your choice will do.

6 steaks, approx 225g (8oz) each
225g (8oz) mushrooms, wiped clean
6 tomatoes
40g (1½oz) butter, melted
salt and black pepper

1 Trim the steaks but leave on a little fat.
2 Thread the mushrooms and tomatoes on to skewers.
3 Brush the steaks and vegetables with the melted butter
and season with the salt and pepper. Grill over charcoal for
between 5 and 15 minutes depending on how you like your
steak cooked. Cook the vegetables on the outside of the fire,
turning frequently. Do not overcook or the tomatoes will fall
off the skewers.
4 Arrange the vegetables around the steaks on a large
serving dish and serve with a pilav or cooked vegetables.

Bistecca alla fiorentina – Italian marinated steak

A traditional Italian dish. Serve with a salad and/or rice dish.

6 T-bone or sirloin steaks, cut about 2.5cm (1in) thick
black pepper
1 teaspoon salt

Marinade
3 tablespoons olive oil
3 tablespoons wine vinegar
2 bay leaves
1 teaspoon thyme
2 cloves garlic, crushed
1 teaspoon oregano
2 tablespoons chopped parsley
150ml (¼ pint) red wine

1 Place the steaks in a large shallow dish. Mix the marinade
ingredients together and pour over the steaks. Turn the
steaks, cover the dish and leave at room temperature for

about 5 hours or in a refrigerator for 8 hours or overnight.
Turn the steaks frequently.

2 Remove the meat from the marinade and pat dry with
kitchen paper. Grind black pepper on to both sides of each
steak. Grill over charcoal, turning occasionally for 5–7
minutes if you like your steak rare, but longer if you prefer
it medium or well done.

3 Transfer the steaks to a serving dish, sprinkle with the
salt and serve.

Cowboy steaks

No explanations are needed here. The name is enough to
conjure up the image of hearty steaks sizzling under the
open sky. I'd love to know how and where they carried all
the spices required!

6 large steaks

Marinade
100g (4oz) bacon dripping
1 large onion, finely chopped
1 clove garlic, crushed
6 tablespoons lemon juice
1½ tablespoons Worcestershire sauce
1½ tablespoons horseradish sauce
1 teaspoon salt
½ teaspoon black pepper
1 teaspoon paprika
4 bay leaves

1 Prepare the marinade by melting the dripping in a frying
pan. Add the onion and fry for several minutes until soft.
Stir in the remaining ingredients and simmer for 2–3
minutes. Allow to cool.

2 Arrange the steaks in a large, shallow dish and pour the
marinade over them. Leave to marinate for 2–3 hours,
turning occasionally.

3 Grill over charcoal for between 8 and 20 minutes
depending on how well done you like your steak.

4 Serve with a corn salad.

Porterhouse steak avec épices

This simple steak recipe is very popular in France. The steak is coated in a butter-spice mixture.

It is ideal on a bed of saffron rice or with a selection of salads.

6 porterhouse steaks, approx 225g (8oz) each

Baste
50g (2oz) butter, melted
1 clove garlic, crushed
1 teaspoon turmeric
1 teaspoon cumin
½ teaspoon cayenne pepper
1 teaspoon salt
½ teaspoon black pepper

Mix all the baste ingredients together in a small bowl until smooth. Brush the steaks on both sides with this mixture. Grill over charcoal, turning frequently and brushing each time with the butter mixture. Cook for 5–7 minutes if you like your steak rare, longer if you prefer it better done.

Steak with barbecue sauce

A simple but delicious steak with barbecue sauce which is fast becoming a classic in the Americas.

6 rump or rib steaks, approx 2–2.5cm (¾–1in) thick

Marinade
150ml (¼ pint) tomato ketchup
60ml (2fl oz) Worcestershire sauce
2 tablespoons mustard (American or English)
1 teaspoon cayenne pepper
1 clove garlic, crushed
salt and pepper to taste
2 tablespoons lemon juice

1 Mix all the marinade ingredients together in a bowl. Place the steaks in a large shallow dish and pour the marinade over them. Turn once and set aside for 1 hour at room temperature.

2 Grill over charcoal, turning occasionally until cooked to your liking.

3 Meanwhile heat the remaining marinade in a saucepan and simmer for a few minutes.

4 Serve the steaks with the marinade sauce and with potatoes and salads.

Sirloin with anchovy

An interesting combination of beef steak with anchovy fillets and stuffed olives. It is pungent, but appetising and will go well with Patates salatasi (page 221) or Mdzhavai (page 218).

1kg (2lb) sirloin steak in one piece cut 3.5cm (1½in) thick
25g (1oz) butter
1 teaspoon anchovy paste
salt and pepper to taste
1 small tin anchovy fillets
handful stuffed green olives
½ teaspoon cumin
3 tablespoons chopped parsley

1 Mix the butter, anchovy paste, salt and pepper until smooth.

2 Place the steak on the charcoal grill and cook without turning for 6–8 minutes. Turn the steak over and spread the uncooked side with half of the anchovy-butter mixture. Cook the remaining side of the steak for a further 6–8 minutes.

3 Place the steak on a large plate, unbuttered side uppermost. Spread the remaining butter-anchovy mixture over the surface of the steak. Arrange the anchovy fillets in a criss-cross pattern across the top of the steak. Place a stuffed olive in the centre of each diamond shape. Sprinkle the cumin and parsley all over the steak and serve immediately. Cut the steak into suitable portions at the table.

Steak with chestnut sauce

This dish uses chestnuts as the basis of the marinade which, with the double cream gives it a very sophisticated flavour.

You can buy puréed chestnuts in most grocers' shops. They usually come in 450g (1lb) cans – buy French or Belgian brands which tend to be the best.

6 rump steaks, abut 225g (8oz) each
25g (1oz) butter
1 clove garlic, crushed
1 onion, finely chopped
4 tablespoons double cream

Marinade
½ teaspoon thyme
½ teaspoon marjoram
175g (6oz) chestnut purée
90ml (3fl oz) Marsala wine
150ml (¼ pint) beef stock
salt and pepper to taste

1 Prepare the marinade by mixing all the ingredients together in a large dish. Add the steaks and turn to coat with the marinade. Set aside for 30 minutes at room temperature.
2 Remove the steaks and reserve the marinade. Grill the steaks over charcoal until cooked to your liking.
3 Meanwhile melt the butter in a small pan, add the garlic and onion and fry until golden. Stir in the remaining marinade and the cream, bring just to the boil and then simmer gently for 3–4 minutes. Serve the steaks on individual plates with the sauce poured over the top of each one.

Black pepper steak

Here are two versions of the famed 'Steak au poivre'. Hot spiced tomatoes add interest to the first dish; the second is marinated in an oil and vinegar marinade. Serve with a rice dish and perhaps a mushroom salad.

6 steaks, approx 225–350g (½–¾lb) each

Version 1
2 tablespoons whole black peppercorns
40g (1½oz) butter

1 clove garlic, crushed
4 large tomatoes, sliced
1 teaspoon salt
6 tablespoons brandy

1 Roughly crush the peppercorns and sprinkle both sides of the meat with them. Set aside for about 1 hour.
2 Grill the steaks over charcoal, turning occasionally until cooked to your liking.
3 Meanwhile melt the butter in a frying pan, add the garlic and fry for 1 minute. Add the tomato slices and sauté until just soft. Sprinkle in the salt.
4 Place the steaks on a large plate and arrange the tomato slices over the top. Warm the brandy, ignite it and spoon, flaming over the meat.

Version 2
240ml (8fl oz) wine vinegar
120ml (4fl oz) oil
50g (2oz) brown sugar
1 teaspoon salt
½ teaspoon marjoram
½ teaspoon rosemary
1 onion, finely chopped
1 clove garlic, finely chopped
3 tablespoons coarsely crushed black peppercorns

1 Combine all the ingredients except the peppercorns in a large bowl. Add the steaks and leave to marinate for 2 hours.
2 Remove the steaks and press the crushed peppercorns over both sides of the steaks.
3 Cook and serve as above.

Pul-ko-kee – Korean grilled beef

The seven basic flavours of Korean food are garlic, ginger, black pepper, spring onions, soy sauce, sesame oil and sesame seeds. Many are present in this popular dish.

1kg (2lb) shoulder or leg of beef, cut into thin slices about 7.5cm (3in) square

Marinade
4 tablespoons sugar
2 tablespoons oil
6 tablespoons soy sauce
½ teaspoon black pepper
1 spring onion, finely chopped
1 clove garlic, crushed
1 tablespoon flour
2 tablespoons prepared sesame seeds (see below)
1 teaspoon salt

1 Place the sugar and oil in a large bowl and mix well. Add
the soy sauce, black pepper, spring onion, garlic and flour
and stir well.
2 To prepare the sesame seeds place about 50g (2oz) sesame
seeds in a small saucepan over a medium heat and let them
brown slowly, stirring constantly. When the seeds are evenly
browned remove them from the heat and place them, with
the salt, in a mortar or in a blender or grinder and pulverize.
Add 2 tablespoons of this mixture to the marinade and stir
well.
3 Add the meat slices, turn to ensure that they are well
coated. Cover and refrigerate for several hours.
4 Lay the meat slices on the grill and cook for a few minutes,
turning frequently.
5 Serve immediately with a plain white rice.

Variation – Ou-sul kui This is tongue kebab. It uses the
same marinade and requires the same method of cooking.
Substitute for the beef about 1kg (2lb) tongue cut into thin
slices.

Chelo kabab barg – beef kebabs with egg yolks

This is the most famous Persian kebab and it is always served
with chelo rice pilav (page 195). Beef is used, but if you
prefer lamb then use shoulder and cut it into 12.5–15cm
(5–6in) long slices which are 1cm (½in) thick.

1kg (2lb) beef steak or lamb shoulder

Marinade
300ml (½ pint) yoghurt
1 large onion, finely chopped
1 teaspoon salt
½ teaspoon black pepper

Garnish
6 egg yolks
6 pats butter
sumac (see page 255)
1 large onion, cut into rings

1 Cut the meat into slices about 12.5–15cm (5in–6in) × 5cm
(2in) and 1cm (½in) thick. Now pound each piece with a
meat mallet until it is about ½cm (¼in) thick. Divide each
piece into two equal portions and arrange in a shallow dish.
2 Mix the marinade ingredients together in a bowl and pour
over the meat. Turn the pieces to coat well and then cover
and refrigerate for 24 hours.
3 When ready to cook, remove one piece of meat at a time
and carefully thread a flat skewer through its length. When
all the meat is skewered cook the kebabs fairly quickly,
turning frequently so that the meat cooks without drying.
4 Transfer two skewers to each plate and slide the meat on
to them. Cover the meat generously with chelo rice pilav
and sprinkle with sumac. Place an egg yolk and a pat of
butter on top of each serving of rice and mix into the rice
until well blended and until the butter has melted.
   Garnish with the onion rings.

Odessa shashlig – beef in a cider marinade

This kebab is marinated in cider (and sometimes beer) and
spices. It was very popular in the Crimea before the
Revolution and I assume that it still is.
   Cider is widely used in the lands around the Black Sea eg
Turkey, Russia and Rumania. I like the touch of apple in
the marinade – so very Russian. Serve it with kasha or rice
pilav of your choice.

1kg (2lb) shoulder of beef, cut into 2.5cm (1in) cubes
button mushrooms
bay leaves

Marinade
150ml (¼ pint) strong cider
1 tablespoon brown sugar
2 tablespoons oil
2 tablespoons vinegar, cider or tarragon vinegar
1 onion, finely chopped
1 small cooking apple, peeled, cored and finely chopped
½ teaspoon dillweed
½ teaspoon tarragon
1 teaspoon salt
½ teaspoon white pepper
½ teaspoon rosemary

1 Place all the marinade ingredients together in a saucepan.
Bring the mixture quickly to the boil then lower the heat
and simmer for 4 minutes. Remove from the heat and set
aside to cool for 15 minutes.
2 Put the cubed meat into a large, shallow dish, pour the
marinade over them and toss well so that the meat is well
coated. Cover and refrigerate for 12–24 hours.
3 Remove from the refrigerator and thread the cubes on
skewers alternating with mushrooms and bay leaves. Cook
over charcoal, turning and basting frequently with the
remaining marinade for 10–15 minutes.

Hamemov davari khorovu – beef with herbs kebab

This Armenian kebab is particularly good with burghul pilav
(page 200) and a bowl of yoghurt-cucumber salad – jajig
(page 212).
   A marinade of different herbs (traditionally they should be
fresh) gives this kebab an almost aromatic flavour.

1kg (2lb) beef, sirloin or fillet, cut 2.5cm (1in) thick

Marinade
75g (3oz) butter or ghee, melted
3 tablespoons chopped spring onions

2 tablespoons chopped chives
4 tablespoons chopped parsley
1 teaspoon dillweed
1 teaspoon oregano
1 teaspoon basil
1 teaspoon marjoram
½ teaspoon cinnamon
½ teaspoon paprika
1 teaspoon salt
juice 1 large lemon

Garnish
fresh tarragon or mint leaves
lemon wedges

1 Put all the marinade ingredients into a bowl and mix well.
2 Cut the beef into 5–7.5cm (2in–3in) pieces. Place in a large
shallow dish and pour in the marinade. Stir to coat all the
pieces and leave for at least 2 hours.
3 Thread onto skewers and grill over charcoal for about 6–8
minutes or until cooked to your liking.
4 Meanwhile heat any remaining marinade in a small
saucepan and simmer for 5 minutes.
5 Serve the kebabs immediately with a little marinade
poured over each one. Garnish.

Satay Daging – Malay beef kebab

A spicy beef kebab from Malaysia which is simple to prepare.
Serve with *kuah saté 1* (page 249) and a fresh vegetable
garnish as well as rice and bread.

1kg (2lb) steak, rump or fillet

Marinade
1 tablespoon turmeric
1 tablespoon cumin
1 tablespoon ground fennel
grated rind 1 lemon
1 teaspoon salt
1 tablespoon brown sugar
30ml (1fl oz) coconut milk (optional; page 251)
about 30ml (1fl oz) warm water

Garnish
onion rings, sliced tomatoes and cucumber
chutney

1 Trim fat from the beef and cut it into thin slices. Cut the
meat into 2.5cm (1in) cubes.
2 Place the marinade ingredients in a shallow dish and stir
until the sugar has dissolved. Add a little more warm water
if necessary. Add the beef cubes, toss until well coated, cover
and refrigerate for 2–3 hours.
3 Thread the pieces of beef on to skewers, alternating them
with thin slices of fat. Cook over charcoal for 6–8 minutes
or until cooked to your liking, turning frequently.
4 Garnish with the vegetables and serve with chutney, rice
and kuah saté 1 (see page 249).

Kingston-style kebabs

An exotic kebab of beef and fruits from the West Indies. It
is popular throughout the Caribbean and especially in
Jamaica.

1kg (2lb) sirloin or tenderloin steak, cut into 2.5cm (1in) cubes
3 ripe bananas
18 cubes fresh or tinned pineapple
18 cubes peeled pawpaw, if available

Marinade
50g (2oz) butter
2 onions, chopped
2 cloves garlic, crushed
2 ripe mangoes or 6–8 ripe apricots
½ teaspoon salt
½ teaspoon cayenne pepper
2 tablespoons curry powder
3 tablespoons vinegar
50g (2oz) brown sugar

1 To prepare the marinade, heat the butter in a saucepan,
add the onion and garlic and fry until golden.
2 Meanwhile peel and stone the mangoes or apricots and
mash the flesh. Add to the saucepan together with

remaining ingredients. Stir until the sugar dissolves and then pour into a shallow dish to cool. Add the meat cubes, toss to coat with the marinade and then cover and refrigerate overnight.

3 Peel the bananas and cut into 2.5cm (1in) pieces.

4 Thread the meat cubes onto skewers alternating them with pieces of banana, pineapple and pawpaw. Reserve any remaining marinade.

5 Grill over charcoal for 6–8 minutes or until cooked to your liking, turning occasionally.

6 Meanwhile heat the remaining marinade in a small pan.

7 Serve the kebabs with a plain rice pilav and use the heated marinade as a sauce.

Saté istimewa – Indonesian-style beef kebab

Saté is the Indonesian equivalent of kebab which, due to climate and customs have become very intricate and exotic. They are normally served with kuah saté 1 or 2 (see page 249), but there is nothing to stop you experimenting with some rice pilavs or cooked vegetables as accompaniments.

1kg (2lb) rump steak, cut into 2.5cm (1in) pieces

Marinade
1 bunch spring onions, finely chopped
2 tablespoons lemon juice
1 tablespoon brown sugar
1 clove garlic, finely chopped
1 teaspoon cumin
240ml (8fl oz) Arak (see page 254 – you can substitute sherry or
  brandy.)
1 teaspoon grated lime peel
3 tablespoons soy sauce
½ teaspoon salt

1 Mix all the marinade ingredients together in a large bowl. Add the pieces of steak, mix well and leave for 4–6 hours.

2 Thread the meat on to skewers and cook over charcoal for 6–8 minutes or until cooked to your liking, turning frequently. Serve with one of the sauces suggested above.

Saté parsi – beef marinated in brandy and sugar

Despite its name – Persian Saté – this kebab is in fact a speciality of Indonesia, although it probably originated with the Parsee, a sect of Persian origin who left their country over a thousand years ago to avoid Islam. That is why pork can be included in this recipe.

450g (1lb) sirloin steak, cut into 1cm (½in) pieces
450g (1lb) lean leg of pork, cut into 1cm (½in) pieces
12 small onions
12 small tomatoes
12 mushrooms, soaked in warm water for 1 hour
2 courgettes, topped and tailed and each cut into 6 rounds

Marinade
1 clove garlic, finely chopped
1 large onion, finely chopped
8 black peppercorns
180ml (6fl oz) Arak (see page 254) or brandy
1 tablespoon brown sugar
1 teaspoon lime peel, chopped
150ml (¼ pint) peanut or vegetable oil
1 teaspoon salt

1 Mix all the marinade ingredients together in a large bowl. Add all the meat pieces, stir, cover and refrigerate for 6–8 hours.
2 Peel the onions and boil in a little water for 5–10 minutes and then drain.
3 Thread the meats and vegetables alternately onto skewers. Cook over charcoal for 8–10 minutes. Remember to check that the pork is cooked.
4 Serve in the traditional manner with kuah saté 1 or 2 (see page 249) and with any remaining marinade, heated through.

Saté madura – beef marinated with coconut and nuts

This saté from Java makes use of coconut, chillies and a local nut called kemiri nut – for which either Brazil nuts or walnuts can be substituted.

1kg (2lb) rumpsteak, cut into 2.5 cm (1in) pieces

Marinade
2 onions, finely chopped
2 cloves garlic, finely chopped
6 Brazil nuts or whole walnuts, finely chopped
4 red chillies, thinly sliced
1 tablespoon coriander
1 teaspoon cumin
½ teaspoon Chinese shrimp sauce, available in all Chinese food
  shops
1 tablespoon brown sugar
1 tablespoon lemon juice
1 tablespoon soy sauce
2 tablespoons oil
50g (2oz) desiccated coconut
½ teaspoon salt

1 Mix all the marinade ingredients together in a large bowl.
Add the meat cubes, stir well and leave at room temperature
for 1–2 hours.
2 Thread the cubes onto skewers and grill over charcoal,
turning frequently for 6–8 minutes or until cooked to your
liking.
3 Serve with any rice dish and kuah saté 1 (see page 249).

Hawaiian beef kebabs

A Hawaiian speciality based on the Japanese teriyaki, but
with more exotic overtones.

1kg (2lb) sirloin steak, cut into 2.5cm (1in) cubes
450g (1lb) cubed fresh or tinned pineapple

Marinade
150ml (¼ pint) soy sauce
2 tablespoons olive oil
2 tablespoons lemon juice
1 clove garlic, crushed
75g (3oz) brown sugar
1 teaspoon fresh ginger, peeled and finely chopped
½ teaspoon salt

1 Mix all the marinade ingredients together in a large bowl. Add the meat and pineapple, mix well, cover and refrigerate for several hours.
2 Thread the meat and pineapple cubes alternately onto skewers. Grill over charcoal for 6–8 minutes or until cooked to your liking, turning regularly.
3 Serve with rice and fresh salads. A special Hawaiian touch is to serve a bright flower impaled on each skewer when serving.

Laham fis-seffud – Maltese beef kebabs

These kebabs make an interesting use of both beef and pork reflecting very clearly the culture of Malta i.e. both its Christian and its Arab background. The name of the dish is of Arab origin.

The use of cubes of bread is also interesting although not original – *Maiale allo spiedo* (page 114) from Italy makes use of bread as well.

1kg (2lb) sirloin steak, cut into 2.5cm (1in) cubes
12 streaky bacon rashers
thick slices white bread, crusts removed, cut into 2.5cm (1in) cubes
12 bay leaves
4 tablespoons melted butter
1 teaspoon cumin
salt and pepper to taste

1 Roll up the bacon rashers.
2 Thread the meat cubes, bacon rolls, bread cubes and bay leaves alternately on to skewers.
3 Stir the cumin into the melted butter and then brush this mixture over the kebabs.
4 Grill over charcoal for 6–8 minutes or until cooked to your liking, turning and basting frequently with the butter mixture.
5 Serve immediately with fried potatoes or on a bed of rice pilav.

Beef Kofta – minced beef kebab with coconut milk sauce

This is a Moghul dish of distinction from India and, in
particular from Hyderabad.

  Usually the meatballs are cooked in the sauce, but in this
recipe the meat is cooked over charcoal and the sauce is
served separately.

1kg (2lb) lean minced beef
4 medium-sized chilli peppers, seeded and finely chopped
1 small onion, finely chopped
1 clove garlic, finely chopped
1 teaspoon salt
½ teaspoon ground black pepper
1 teaspoon cinnamon
1 egg
plain flour

Sauce
50g (2oz) ghee or butter
1 large onion, thinly sliced
1 tablespoon garam masala
450ml (¾ pint) coconut milk (page 251)
juice 1 large lemon

1 Place the meat, chilli peppers, onion, garlic, salt, pepper
and cinnamon in a large bowl and knead until the mixture
is smooth. Break the egg into a small bowl, whisk and add
to the meat mixture. Knead the mixture for a further
minute or two.
2 Sprinkle a little flour onto your hands and onto the work
top. Divide the mixture into walnut-sized pieces and roll
between your floured palms into small balls. Set aside at
room temperature for 30–45 minutes.
3 Meanwhile prepare the sauce by melting the ghee or butter
in a saucepan. Add the onion and garam masala and cook
for about 5 minutes, stirring frequently. Gradually add the
coconut milk and simmer gently for a further 5 minutes.
Add a little of the lemon juice, taste and add more if
necessary.
4 Thread the meatballs on to skewers and cook over charcoal
for about 10 minutes, turning frequently. Serve the kebabs

on a bed of saffron rice. Pour the coconut-sauce over the meat and serve.

Ploeskavice – Serbian beef and pork kebab

A typical minced kebab from Yugoslavia. There are many such recipes throughout the Balkans where beef and pork are often mixed, as are lamb and pork.

This is a skewered version but the mixture is often simply flattened and grilled like a hamburger.

Serve with a pilav, salads and pickles.

450 (1lb) lean beef, minced twice
350g (¾lb) lean pork, minced twice
½ teaspoon black pepper
1 teaspoon salt
1 red pepper, seeded and very finely chopped
2 tablespoons finely chopped parsley or chervil

Sauce
50g (2oz) butter
2 tablespoons lemon juice
2 teaspoons chopped parsley
2 teaspoons marjoram
1 teaspoon paprika
1 teaspoon salt

Garnish
fresh tarragon leaves
spring onions and radishes

1 Place the meats in a large bowl and add the black pepper, salt, red pepper and parsley or chervil. Knead for about 5 minutes or until smooth. Divide the mixture into 12 portions. Dampen your hands and shape each portion around a skewer making a thin sausage about 15cm (6in) long. Moisten your hands frequently to ease the shaping of the kebabs.
2 Grill over charcoal, turning frequently for 12–15 minutes or until the kebabs are cooked through.
3 Meanwhile make the sauce by melting the butter in a small saucepan. Add the remaining ingredients and stir well.

4 Serve the kebabs immediately with the garnishes. Pour a
little of the butter-lemon sauce over each kebab.

Kebab kurdi – Kurdish kebab with hot sauce

This recipe from Kurdistan is for people who like hot food.
The quantities of chilli pepper and fresh chillies can be
varied according to taste.
  Serve with a rice or burghul pilav.

750g (1½lb) lamb or beef, minced twice
75g (3oz) fresh breadcrumbs
1 onion, coarsely chopped
3 tablespoons chopped parsley
1 egg
1 teaspoon salt
1½ teaspoons chilli pepper
2 large green peppers, seeded and cut into 2.5cm (1in) squares

Sauce
3 tablespoons oil
1 large onion, finely chopped
25g (1oz) plain flour
2–3 chilli peppers, seeded and thinly sliced
4 large ripe tomatoes, blanched and peeled OR 1 × 450g (1lb) tin
  tomatoes
1 tablespoon tomato purée diluted in 4 tablespoons warm water
300ml (½ pint) water
1 teaspoon salt

Garnish
fresh mint or tarragon leaves

1 Place the minced meat, breadcrumbs, onion and parsley in
a large bowl and knead vigorously until well blended. Add
the egg, salt and chilli pepper and knead for a further 2–3
minutes. Keeping your hands damp with warm water form
the mixture into walnut-sized balls. Thread on to skewers
alternating with pieces of pepper. Refrigerate for 30
minutes.
2 Meanwhile prepare the sauce by heating the oil in a
saucepan and frying the onion until soft. Stir in the flour

and then add the chilli peppers, chopped tomatoes, diluted
tomato purée, water and salt. Bring to the boil stirring
constantly and then lower the heat and simmer for about 10
minutes. Keep warm.

3 Grill the kebabs over charcoal for about 10–12 minutes
until cooked through. Serve with the garnishes and with a
little hot sauce poured over each.

Churrasco misto – Brazilian mixed kebab

In Brazil and Argentina this mixed kebab is very popular. A
particular ingredient always included is a local sausage
chorizo made from a mixture of pork and beef. You can find
these in continental shops and on delicatessen counters in
many supermarkets. However, you can use ordinary pork
sausages instead.

450g (1lb) rump or fillet steak, cut into 5cm (2in) cubes
350g (¾lb) lean pork, cut into 5cm (2in) cubes
6 pork sausages, each twisted in half OR sufficient chorizos to give
  12 × 5cm (2in) pieces
6 small onions
12 button mushrooms, wiped clean
6 small tomatoes

Baste
3 tablespoons oil
3 tablespoons vinegar
2 tablespoons finely chopped parsley
2 teaspoons paprika
1 crushed bay leaf
1 teaspoon salt
½ teaspoon black pepper

Garnish
lemon wedges

1 Thread the cubed meats on to 6 skewers.
2 Thread the sausage pieces and vegetables on to 6 more
skewers.
3 Mix the baste ingredients together in a small bowl. Brush
all the kebabs with this baste and grill over charcoal for

12–15 minutes, turning and brushing frequently with the baste. Make sure that the pork is cooked through before serving.

Sirdi khorovu – beef heart kebab with aubergines and courgettes

This Armenian recipe can also be made with lamb's hearts. Aubergines and courgettes cooked over charcoal taste delicious. Served with pitta bread, pickles, olives and fresh salad, this kebab makes an excellent meal.

1kg (2lb) beef heart
2 long aubergines, cut into 2cm (¾in) thick rounds
3 courgettes, cut into 2cm (¾in) thick rounds

Marinade
1 teaspoon chilli powder
2 teaspoons salt
2 cloves garlic, crushed
3 spring onions, thinly sliced
½ teaspoon black pepper
150ml (¼ pint) oil
150ml (¼ pint) red wine
2 bay leaves

Garnish
lemon wedges
olives, radishes etc

1 Wash and clean the heart and remove any fat and tubes. Cut the meat into 2.5cm (1in) cubes.
2 Mix all the marinade ingredients together in a large bowl. Add the beef cubes, stir well, cover and refrigerate overnight.
3 Thread the cubes on to skewers alternating them with aubergine and courgette slices. Grill over charcoal for 12–15 minutes, turning frequently. Serve with the garnishes.

Anticuchos – Peruvian beef heart kebab

This charming kebab is sold throughout Peru by street vendors.

Ox hearts make excellent kebabs, but you can very satisfactorily substitute lamb's hearts if you wish.
Serve with a rice pilav, fresh salad and pickles.

1kg (2lb) ox heart

Marinade
180ml (6fl oz) vinegar
2 cloves garlic, crushed
2 dried hot chillies, crushed OR 1 tablespoon chilli powder
½ teaspoon cumin
1½ teaspoon salt
2 tablespoons finely chopped fresh coriander.

Sauce
1 teaspoon Worcestershire sauce
1 tablespoon tomato purée
1 tablespoon oil
½ teaspoon black pepper

1 Mix the marinade ingredients together in a shallow bowl.
2 Thoroughly wash the heart and remove and discard the fat and tubes. Cut the meat into 2.5cm (1in) cubes. Add to the marinade, mix well, cover and refrigerate for at least 12 hours.
3 Thread the meat on to skewers and reserve the marinade
4 Mix the sauce ingredients together in a small bowl and add about 90ml (3fl oz) of the marinade.
5 Grill the kebabs over charcoal for 10–12 minutes, turning and basting frequently with the sauce. Serve immediately.

Heart kebabs

These are delicious especially when accompanied by a light salad and some pitta or lavash bread.

1.5kg (3lb) beef heart

Marinade
1 teaspoon chilli pepper
2 teaspoons salt
2 cloves garlic, crushed
3 spring onions, thinly sliced

½ teaspoon black pepper
150ml (¼ pint) oil
150ml (¼ pint) red wine
2 bay leaves

Garnish
lemon wedges

1 Wash and clean the heart and remove all the fat and tubes.
Cut the meat into 2.5cm (1in) cubes.
2 Mix all the marinade ingredients in a large bowl, add the
meat cubes and stir well. Cover and refrigerate overnight.
3 Thread the meat on to skewers and grill over charcoal for
10–12 minutes, turning frequently. Serve immediately with
the lemon wedges.

Saté hati sapi – ox liver and heart saté

The red chillies give this dish an extra dimension.

450g (1lb) ox liver, cut into 2.5cm (1in) pieces
450g (1lb) ox heart, cut into 2.5cm (1in) pieces

Marinade
1 large onion, finely chopped
4 good sized red chillies, sliced
2 cloves garlic, finely chopped
4 tablespoons ketjap manis (page 254 or use 1 teaspoon honey mixed
  with 4 tablespoons soy-bean sauce)
1 tablespoon lemon juice
1 tablespoon brown sugar
3 tablespoons peanut oil or vegetable oil
1½ teaspoons salt

1 Mix all the marinade ingredients together in a large bowl.
Add the ox liver pieces and marinate at room temperature
for 3–5 hours. Refrigerate the liver pieces.
2 When ready to cook thread the heart and liver pieces
alternately on to skewers. Cook over charcoal, turning and
basting frequently with the remaining marinade for 10–15
minutes.
3 Serve with a plain rice pilav and Kuah Saté 1 or 2 (see
page 249).

Brochettes italiennes – liver and sausage kebab

This is an unusual and exceptionally tasty kebab that consists of bite-sized pieces of liver, chipolata sausage, mushrooms and tomatoes. Serve on a bed of rice, accompanied by a mixed salad.

750g (1½lb) calf's liver, cut into 2.5cm (1in) cubes
450g (1lb) chipolata sausages or cocktail sausages
225g (8oz) button mushrooms, wiped clean
6 large tomatoes, quartered
12 bay leaves

Marinade
100g (4oz) butter, melted
1 teaspoon black pepper
1 teaspoon cumin

1 Mix the marinade ingredients in a bowl, add the liver pieces and stir well.
2 If using chipolata sausages twist each one in half to form smaller ones.
3 Thread the liver pieces, sausages, mushrooms, tomato quarters and bay leaves on to skewers and grill for about 10 minutes, turning and brushing frequently with the butter mixture. Serve immediately.

Veal kebab with cabbage salad

A charming veal kebab with a cabbage salad dressed with yoghurt and mayonnaise. Serve with a rice pilav or potatoes – preferably roast.

750g (1½lb) white cabbage
6 tablespoons mayonnaise
1kg (2lb) fillet of veal, cut into 2.5cm (1in) cubes

Marinade
300ml (½ pint) yoghurt
1 onion, thinly sliced
juice 1 lemon
½ teaspoon ground ginger
½ teaspoon turmeric

1 teaspoon coriander
1 teaspoon salt
¼ teaspoon black pepper

Garnish
lemon wedges
radishes

1 Remove damaged outer leaves of the cabbage and discard.
Also remove the thick core – you can eat this by slicing it
thinly and dipping it in salt – delicious! Shred the cabbage
leaves very thinly, transfer to a colander, wash under cold
running water and leave to drain.
2 Mix all the marinade ingredients together.
3 Place the veal cubes in a large bowl, pour over half the
marinade and toss well. Cover and refrigerate for 3–4 hours.
4 Stir the remaining marinade into the mayonnaise and
refrigerate.
5 Thread the meat on to skewers and cook over charcoal for
10–12 minutes, turning and basting with its marinade
frequently.
6 Meanwhile place the shredded cabbage in a large bowl,
add the mayonnaise-marinade dressing and mix thoroughly.
7 To serve, arrange the cabbage salad on a large platter and
place the kebabs on top. Garnish with the lemon wedges
and radishes and serve immediately.

Veal in yoghurt

This light and extremely tasty veal kebab makes use of a
yoghurt marinade.

1kg (2lb) shoulder of veal, cut into 2.5cm (1in) cubes
3 onions, quartered
2 green peppers, seeded and cut into 2.5cm (1in) pieces

Marinade
300ml (½ pint) yoghurt
1 clover garlic, crushed
1 large onion, finely chopped
1 teaspoon salt
¼ teaspoon black pepper

Garnish
1 teaspoon chilli pepper

1 Mix all the marinade ingredients together in a large bowl.
Add the meat cubes, toss to coat, cover and refrigerate for
4–6 hours.
2 Thread the meat on to skewers, alternating with onion
quarters and pieces of green pepper. Reserve the marinade.
Grill the kebabs for 10–15 minutes, turning frequently.
3 When almost ready to serve heat the reserved marinade
in a small pan.
4 Serve the kebabs on a large plate with the chilli pepper
sprinkled over them and with the warmed sauce as an
accompaniment.

Davari shishlig – Armenian veal kebab with courgettes and
tomatoes

Veal is not much used in the Middle East or, for that matter
in the Far East. This Armenian recipe is an exception. It is
also known as Ani Khorovadze – a favourite of the city of
Ani.
  It should be served with fresh tarragon, parsley and spring
onions.

1kg (2lb) shoulder of veal, cut into 2.5cm (1in) cubes
450g (1lb) courgettes, topped, tailed and cut into 2.5cm (1in) rounds
12 small tomatoes

Marinade
150ml (¼ pint) oil
90ml (3fl oz) red wine vinegar
1 teaspoon salt
½ teaspoon black pepper
1 teaspoon cumin

Garnish
3 tablespoons sumac (page 255)

1 Mix the marinade ingredients together in a large bowl.
Add the meat cubes, stir well, cover and leave to marinate
at room temperature for 4–6 hours or refrigerate overnight.

2 Thread the meat on to skewers alternating the cubes with courgette slices and tomatoes. Grill over charcoal, turning frequently for 10–15 minutes.
3 Serve on a bed of rice pilav with vermicelli (page 201) and with the sumac sprinkled over the top.

Fatányéros – 'Wooden platter' kebabs

The name comes from the simple wooden plate cut from a tree trunk on which the meal used to be served.

The meal is, in reality, a charcoal-cooked mixed grill. If you feel that the quantities are too large then simply eliminate whatever you wish. Serve with chipped potatoes.

6 veal cutlets
6 small pieces rump steak
6 small pork chops
6 rashers bacon
350g (¾lb) chicken or goose livers
4 tablespoons melted butter

To serve
Chipped potatoes

1 Place all the meats on a rack over a charcoal grill, putting the thickest pieces over the hottest part of the fire. Turn and brush with the melted butter frequently.
2 While the meat is cooking, fry the potatoes.
3 When all the meats are cooked arrange them around the edge of a platter and pile the chips into the centre. Serve with a mixed salad and relishes.

Nanor – veal chops in wine and herbs

'Even a worm in a rock loves herbs' – Persian saying

This dish is usually accompanied by a garnish of wild herbs. Unfortunately most of these herbs are of Caucasian origin and are extremely difficult to find fresh in Europe. I have therefore suggested some that are more easily available and perfectly acceptable e.g. parsley, mint, cress, dill, coriander, tarragon, chervil, basil etc.

6 veal chops, about 2.5cm (1in) thick
4 tablespoons melted butter

Marinade
300ml (½ pint) dry white wine
1 tablespoon paprika
1 teaspoon salt

To serve
sumac (see page 255)
6 thin slices lemon
selection of fresh herbs

1 Mix the marinade ingredients together in a shallow dish.
Add the veal chops, turn once and leave to stand for 1–2 hours
at room temperature, turning occasionally.
2 When ready to cook, brush each chop with the butter and
place on the grill. Cook for about 15 minutes, turning and
brushing with the butter frequently.
3 Serve with a little sumac sprinkled on each chop, a slice
of lemon and some mixed fresh herbs.

Barbecued veal chops

An extremely simple but tasty method of preparing veal
chops.

6 large veal chops

Marinade
1 onion, finely chopped
1 clove garlic, finely chopped
1 teaspoon coriander
½ teaspoon chilli pepper
1 tablespoon chopped parsley
1 teaspoon oregano
1 teaspoon salt
6 tablespoons oil
3 tablespoons malt vinegar

1 Mix all the marinade ingredients together in a large
shallow dish. Add the chops, turn once and leave at room
temperature for 3–5 hours, turning frequently.

2 Cook the chops over charcoal for 12–15 minutes or until cooked to your liking, turning and basting frequently with the marinade.

Burgers, frankfurters and sausages

Frankfurters, hot-dogs, hamburgers, beefburgers, sausages etc. all make tasty barbecues. Grill them, turning at least once and then serve as you like with vegetables, salads, pilavs or bread. Sausages require the same cooking time as the meat they contain. Frankfurters are pre-cooked and so need only a few minutes warming through. Remember to prick all sausages to prevent their bursting.

You can cook them as they come or use any of the bastes in the section on Marinades.

However, if you wish to make life more difficult but fulfilling and if perhaps you are, like me, not much taken with the bland burgers available in our shops, then below there is a recipe for basic burgers. This is a tasty recipe, but you can and indeed should experiment by trying the addition of different herbs and spices, e.g. soy sauce, garlic, mustard, ginger, parsley, chilli pepper etc.

1kg (2lb) minced beef
1 large onion, finely chopped
3 teaspoons salt
½ teaspoon black pepper
3 tablespoons Worcestershire sauce

1 Place all the ingredients together in a large bowl and knead for several minutes until the mixture is well blended and smooth.
2 Divide the mixture into 6 portions and shape into burgers about 1cm (½in) thick.
3 Grill over charcoal for 8–10 minutes, turning occasionally.
4 Serve with pilavs and salads and/or vegetables or in a toasted bun.

You can further enhance the flavour of the burger by adding a topping, e.g.:
(a) cheese – shortly after turning for the last time top with

a slice of cheese and continue to cook until the cheese begins to melt.

(b) dill sauce – mix together 1 tablespoon dill seed, 90ml (3fl oz) yoghurt or soured cream, ½ teaspoon mustard and ½ teaspoon paprika. Spoon some of this sauce on each burger when you serve it.

(c) cheese and bacon filling – shortly after turning for the last time sprinkle the burgers with grated cheese e.g. cheddar, blue cheese etc. Grill 3 rashers of bacon until crisp, chop and sprinkle over the melting cheese

(3) onion – slice a large onion into rings, grill until golden and place on top of the burgers.

You can also, of course top the burgers with pickles and relishes, grilled mushrooms, sliced tomatoes etc.

Pork kebabs

'Look at Pork, there's a subject. If you want a subject, look at pork'
– Charles Dickens

Most pigs are slaughtered young due to the great demand for
lean pork. Pork is fat and firm and has more red meat than
white. It is more difficult to digest than lamb or beef. It is
eaten either fresh or cured and is particularly good when
salted and smoked.

In Europe pork used to be sold in the winter months only,
as it was thought not to be suitable for the warmer months.
In the Middle East and other 'Islamic' countries it is not
eaten at all. The nutritional habits of the pig and the idea
that pork cannot withstand warm temperatures have created
the religious concepts of dirt and ugliness. However, today
most pigs are bred in modern, sanitary conditions.

When buying pork look for meat that is pinkish-grey and
lean with streaks of white fat running through it. The outer
layer of fat should not be too thick and should look creamy-
white. All pork joints can be roasted, remember that pork
has more flavour if cooked on the bone. One note of warning
– pork must be cooked until it is **well done**. This is because
the muscles of the animal might be infested with the parasite
trichinia – which does not usually affect the hog (lucky
hog!), but could cause trichinosis in humans.

Suckling pig – ideal for large parties. They usually weigh
about 6–8 kg (12–18lb) and are around 3 weeks old. They
are fed only on their mother's milk and have a delicious
flavour.

Leg – usually weigh 5–6 kg (10–12lb) and can be barbecued whole or cut up into steaks etc.

Ham – this comes from the hind leg and is 'dry cured', while gammon is 'wet cured' in a brine solution.

Loin – the best and most expensive joint. It is extremely tender, juicy and lean. A whole loin weighs 6–7.5kg (12–15lb).

Spare ribs – (not to be confused with spare-rib chops) are the rib and breastbones and full of lean, juicy meat. They come from the lower part of the centre section and are excellent for barbecues.

Chops – the tastiest are sirloin pork chops cut from the front portion of the sirloin roast. Loin chops are equally delicious and are cut from the front portion of the centre loin.

Suckling pig

One of the great classics of all time and highly prized since the glorious orgies of Rome.

This dish is very popular in Eastern Europe, especially in Russia and Rumania where the main attraction on Christmas Day is inevitably a succulent pig sometimes still roasted over an open fire.

Most are now cooked in the oven, but if you wish to try one over an open fire then try the recipe below either with or without one of the suggested stuffings.

6–9kg (12–18lb) suckling pig
1½ teaspoons salt
1½ teaspoons black pepper
butter or lard and olive oil
melted butter for basting

1 Ask your butcher to prepare the pig for you. Then singe off any remaining hair or bristle and wash inside and out. Rub the animal all over with the salt and pepper. Rub the inside with butter or lard and brush the outside with the oil. Score the outside skin evenly to make crackling.

2 Truss the legs together and protect the lower parts from burning by covering them with foil. Push the spit through the pig from breast to the hindquarters.

3 Roast for about 3 hours turning frequently and basting with the melted butter. Test if it is cooked by sticking a knitting needle in it – if it penetrates easily then it is ready. Remove the pig from the spit and lay it on a large tray garnished with lettuce leaves, sliced tomatoes etc. Alternatively serve on a bed of rice or, as in Russia, on a bed of kasha (page 202). Place an apple in its mouth and serve immediately.

Serves about 12–15 people.

Below are some recipes for stuffing. Remember that if you stuff the pig you will be able to feed more people but it will take longer to cook.

Noodle stuffing
450g (1lb) noodles – any standard type will do
liver and heart of the pig
25g (1oz) butter
1 onion, finely chopped
1 teaspoon salt
½ teaspoon black pepper

1 Bring a large pan three-quarters filled with lightly salted water to the boil. Add the noodles and cook for 5–7 minutes or until just tender. Strain the noodles into a colander, rinse under cold water and leave to drain.

2 Meanwhile boil the liver and heart in a little water for 10 minutes and then drain. Slice thinly when cool.

3 Heat the butter in a frying pan, add the onion and fry until soft. Add the liver and heart and fry gently for 5 minutes. Transfer to a large bowl, add the noodles and season with the salt and pepper. Mix well and then stuff the pig with this mixture. Sew up the belly and roast.

Caribbean stuffing
450g (1lb) fresh breadcrumbs
4 tablespoons rum
4 tablespoons lard
1 onion, finely chopped

1 clove garlic, finely chopped
1 tablespoon ground ginger
¼ teaspoon nutmeg
1 teaspoon salt
½ teaspoon black pepper
50g (2oz) raisins
1 tablespoon Worcestershire sauce

1 Place the breadcrumbs in a large bowl and moisten with
the rum.
2 Heat the lard in a frying pan, add the onion and garlic
and fry gently until soft. Stir in the moistened breadcrumbs,
ginger, nutmeg, salt and pepper. Cook over a very low heat
for about 5 minutes, stirring occasionally. Remove from the
heat and stir in the raisins and Worcestershire sauce. Stuff
the pig, sew up the belly and roast.
3 When serving arrange plantains, peppers and pineapples
around the dish.

Sausagemeat and apricot stuffing
2 tablespoons oil
3 spring onions, trimmed and chopped
4 cloves garlic, crushed
750g (1½lb) sausagemeat
2 tablespoons chopped fresh chives OR 1 tablespoon dried chives
2 tablespoons chopped fresh sage OR 1 tablespoon dried sage
2 tablespoons fresh thyme OR 1 tablespoon dried thyme
175g (6oz) long grain rice, washed thoroughly and drained
1 teaspoon salt
450g (1lb) tin apricots, drained and with 60ml (2fl oz) juice reserved
grated rind 1 orange

1 Heat the oil in a large frying pan, add the onions and
garlic and fry until soft. Add the sausagemeat, herbs, rice
and salt and cook, stirring frequently for about 5 minutes.
Add the apricots, quartered, reserved juice and the orange
rind and mix well. Stuff the pig, sew up the opening and
roast.
3 When serving, garnish by placing an apple in the pig's
mouth and arranging parsley, orange and apple slices and
grapes around the edge of the large dish. Serve with apple
sauce (see page 253) if desired.

Barbecued leg of pork

Ideal for 8–10 people.
It is simply delicious, full of flavour and with a marvellous aroma that lingers for hours.

Ask your butcher to bone and roll the leg for you.

1 boned and rolled leg of pork, about 5kg (10lb)

Marinade
600ml (1 pint) cider
juice 1 large lemon
juice 1 large orange or grapefruit
4–5 tablespoons wine vinegar
1 teaspoon salt
½ teaspoon black pepper
1 teaspoon paprika
½ teaspoon chilli pepper
1 teaspoon marjoram OR basil OR oregano

1 Mix all the marinade ingredients together in a large bowl. Add the leg of pork and turn to coat well. Cover the bowl and refrigerate for 12–24 hours, turning occasionally.
2 Remove the leg and score the skin evenly so that it will form crackling. Mount on the spit and cook over medium-hot coals, turning and brushing frequently with the remaining marinade. Allow for about 30 minutes per 450g (1lb) and check before serving that it really is cooked through. Serve with rice and salads or vegetables of your choice.

Hawaiian-style leg of pork

The meat is marinated in an interesting apple-soy sauce mixture.

1 boned and rolled leg of pork, about 5kg (10lb)

Marinade
apple sauce – see page 253
300ml (½ pint) dry white wine
300ml (½ pint) soy sauce
2 tablespoons oil

1 large onion, finely chopped
2 cloves garlic, finely chopped
1 teaspoon ground ginger
1 teaspoon turmeric

1 Score the outside skin evenly to form crackling.
2 Mix all the marinade ingredients together in a large bowl,
add the leg of pork and turn to coat well. Cover and
refrigerate for about 8 hours or overnight, turning
occasionally.
3 Thread the leg on to the spit and cook, turning and basting
frequently with remaining marinade. Allow about 30
minutes for each 450g (1lb) and make sure before serving
that it is cooked through.
   Heat any remaining marinade and serve with the pork.

Gerassov Khoz – pork with cherries

'There are young men with red earrings in the fields'

This Armenian kebab makes use of the large sweet cherries
abundant in that land. It is traditionally served with a rice
or burghul pilav, but it can just as easily and successfully be
accompanied by roast or jacket potatoes and a salad of your
choice.

6 large loin pork chops
1 teaspoon salt
½ teaspoon black pepper
1 small onion, thinly sliced
1 tablespoon oil

Marinade
450g (1lb) large black cherries, stoned and with 100g (4oz) squeezed
   to obtain their juice *OR* 450g (1lb) tin Morello cherries, drained
   and with 6 tablespoons of the juice reserved
3 tablespoons Marsala or brandy
6 spring onions, trimmed and finely chopped
4 parsley stalks
1cm (½in) piece fresh ginger, peeled and finely chopped or 1
   teaspoon ground ginger

1 Place the chops on a board and rub the salt and pepper into both sides of each. Arrange in a shallow dish and cover with the onion slices.
2 Mix the cherry juice and other marinade ingredients together in a small bowl and spoon over the chops. Set aside to marinate for 1–2 hours, turning occasionally.
3 Remove the chops and pat dry with kitchen paper. Reserve the marinade. Brush the chops with the oil and then grill for 20–30 minutes, turning occasionally.
4 Meanwhile strain the marinade and discard the onions and parsley stalks. Heat the marinade, with the cherries added, bring to the boil and simmer while you arrange the pork chops on a large dish. Pour the sauce over the chops and serve immediately.

Kaduckievap – pork chops with liver and bacon

This famed kebab from Yugoslavia is one of the national dishes of that country, derived, no doubt, from the time when the country was part of the Ottoman Empire. It is a very substantial dish – along the lines of a charcoal mixed grill. If you feel there is too much then you can always omit some of the meats.

6 pork chops
6 pieces lamb's liver
12 rashers streaky bacon
6 pork sausages
175g (6oz) cheddar or gruyère cheese, cut into 6 pieces
175g (6oz) cream cheese

Baste
3 tablespoons oil
½ teaspoon thyme
½ teaspoon tarragon
2 teaspoons finely chopped parsley
2 green chillies, seeded and finely chopped
½ teaspoon fennel

1 Mix the baste ingredients together in a small bowl. Brush all the meat, including bacon and sausages, all over with

the mixture and lay them on the grill. Put the chops and liver over the hottest part of the fire and arrange the bacon and sausages around the edge. Cook, turning and basting frequently for 20–30 minutes or until the chops are cooked through.

2 Just before serving slit the sausages lengthways and insert a piece of cheddar or gruyère cheese in each and spread each piece of liver with some of the cream cheese. Continue cooking for 1–2 minutes or until the cheese begins to melt.

3 Serve immediately with fresh salads, radishes and spring onions.

Rochester gammon

Succulent gammon steaks with a fragrant and refreshing orange sauce. Serve with potatoes and an okra or aubergine vegetable dish.

6 gammon steaks
1 teaspoon marjoram

Sauce
240ml (8fl oz) dry white wine
150ml (5fl oz) fresh orange juice
25g (1oz) butter
25g (1oz) plain flour
½ teaspoon salt
¼ teaspoon white pepper
grated rind 1 large orange

Garnish
1 large orange, peeled, white pith discarded, thinly sliced

1 Rub the steaks with the marjoram, place on the grill and cook for 10–12 minutes, depending on thickness.

2 Meanwhile prepare the sauce by placing the wine and orange juice in a small saucepan and bringing to the boil. Remove from the heat and set aside. Melt the butter in a small pan, remove from the heat and stir in the flour to make a smooth paste. Gradually add the wine and orange juice, stirring constantly to avoid lumps. Season with the salt and pepper and stir in the orange rind. Return the pan

to the heat and cook, still stirring constantly, for 2–3 minutes or until the sauce is smooth and has thickened. Remove from the heat.

3 Place the steaks on a serving dish and pour the sauce over the top. Garnish with the orange slices and serve.

Brochettes de porc – pork kebab à la provençale

Chunks of pork marinated and grilled until well done are simple and beautiful, as is this French recipe.
 Serve with potatoes and a bowl of fresh salad.

1kg (2lb) lean loin or fillet of pork, cut into 2.5cm (1in) cubes

Marinade
6 tablespoons oil
6 tablespoons vinegar
1 teaspoon salt
½ teaspoon black pepper
2 tablespoons chopped fresh rosemary OR 2 teaspoons dried
  rosemary

1 Mix the marinade ingredients together in a large, shallow dish. Add the pork cubes and turn until completely coated. Leave to marinate at room temperature for at least 6 hours, turning occasionally.

2 Thread on to skewers and cook for about 20 minutes, turning occasionally until cooked through. Serve immediately.

Carne lo espeto – Portuguese kebab

Succulent pieces of pork and lamb marinated in garlic, herbs and sherry. Very popular in the south of the country.

450g (1lb) pork fillet, cut into 2.5cm (1in) cubes
450g (1lb) boned lean shoulder lamb, cut into 2.5cm (1in) cubes

Marinade
4 cloves garlic, crushed
1 tablespoon paprika
1 teaspoon oregano

1 tablespoon grated orange rind
1 teaspoon salt
½ teaspoon black pepper
1 teaspoon sugar
1 tablespoon finely chopped fresh mint OR 1 teaspoon dried mint
3 tablespoons oil
3 tablespoons dry sherry

1 Mix all the marinade ingredients together in a large bowl. Add the meat cubes and turn until thoroughly coated. Set aside for at least 2 hours at room temperature, turning occasionally.
2 Thread alternate pieces of pork and lamb on to skewers and reserve the marinade.
3 Grill over charcoal for 15–20 minutes or until the pork is cooked through, turning and basting frequently with the marinade.

Ražnjići – Serbian-style kebab

These are Yugoslavian veal and pork kebabs. They are one of the great snack dishes of the country.
  Serve with jacket potatoes, salad and cooked vegetables.

450g (1lb) lean veal, cut into 2.5cm (1in) pieces
450g (1lb) pork fillet, cut into 2.5cm (1in) pieces

Marinade
60ml (2fl oz) oil
60ml (2fl oz) dry white wine
1 teaspoon salt
½ teaspoon black pepper
2 teaspoons paprika

Garnish
1 medium onion, finely chopped

1 Mix the marinade ingredients together in a large shallow dish. Add the meat cubes and toss to coat thoroughly. Set aside at room temperature for 2 hours, turning occasionally.
2 Thread the pork and veal pieces alternately on to skewers and reserve the marinade. Grill over charcoal for 15–20

minutes or until the pork is cooked through, turning and brushing frequently with the marinade.
3 Serve the kebabs on a large dish sprinkled with the chopped onion.

Maiale allo spiedo – skewered pork

This recipe is from Southern Italy.
  Serve with a rice pilav or noodles and a salad.

1kg (2lb) fillet or shoulder of pork
stale bread
225g (8oz) sliced prosciutto or gammon
bay leaves
olive oil
salt and pepper

Garnish
watercress

1 Cut the pork into 24 pieces. Cut the stale bread into the same number of similar sized pieces 1cm (½in) thick. Cut the prosciutto or gammon into pieces. Thread the pork and bread alternately on to skewers interspersing them with bay leaves and pieces of prosciutto or gammon. Brush all over with the oil and season with the salt and pepper. Grill over charcoal for about 20 minutes or until the pork is cooked through and the bread is crisp.
2 Arrange on a serving dish and garnish with sprigs of watercress.

Saté Bali – pork kebabs coated with peanuts

An exotic tasting kebab from the Far East. The kebabs are marinated in tabasco and chutney and then rolled in peanuts.
  Serve as an appetizer or, with a plain rice pilav, as a main meal.

1kg (2lb) boned loin of pork, cut into 2.5cm (1in) cubes
100g (4oz) salted peanuts, finely chopped

Marinade
6 tablespoons chutney, preferably mango
1 tablespoon tabasco
1 tablespoon soy sauce
2 tablespoons oil

1 Chop the chutney finely and place in a large bowl with remaining marinade ingredients. Add the meat cubes and toss until well coated. Cover and refrigerate for at least 8 hours or overnight.
2 Thread on to skewers and grill over charcoal for about 15–20 minutes or until cooked through, turning frequently.
3 Spread the chopped peanuts over a large plate. Before serving the saté, roll each kebab in the peanuts making sure that all sides of each meat cube are coated. Serve immediately.

Chaah sieu – Chinese pork kebabs

A tasty kebab from Peking which is simple to prepare.

1kg (2lb) boned loin of pork

Marinade
2 tablespoons sugar
1 teaspoon salt
½ teaspoon black pepper
4 tablespoons soy sauce
2 tablespoons dry sherry

1 Cut the pork into 3.5cm (1½in) cubes and place in a large bowl. Sprinkle the sugar, salt and pepper over the meat and rub well in with your hands. Cover and refrigerate for about 3 hours.
2 Mix the soy sauce and sherry together, pour over the meat and toss until well coated. Refrigerate for a further 3 hours, turning occasionally.
3 Thread on to skewers and cook over charcoal for about 30 minutes or until the meat is cooked through.
  Serve with boiled rice and a fresh salad.

Variation

In the following Chinese recipe from Nankin the marinade is different, but the cooking procedure remains the same.

1kg (2lb) boned loin of pork, cut into 1cm (½ in) cubes

Marinade
1 level teaspoon dry mustard
½ teaspoon ginger
1 small onion, finely chopped
1 clove garlic, finely chopped
4 tablespoons lemon juice
2 tablespoons honey
1 teaspoon salt
½ teaspoon black pepper

1 Mix all the marinade ingredients together in a large bowl, add the meat, mix well, cover and refrigerate for at least 6 hours. Cook as the Chaah Sieu above. Serve with plain boiled rice and an orange or apple and celery salad.

Caribbean pork kebab

An exotic kebab of pork, pineapple, banana and pawpaw (if available) from the Islands in the sun.

1kg (2lb) pork fillet, cut into 2.5cm (1in) cubes
2 firm bananas, cut into 3.5cm (1½in) pieces
18 2.5–3.5cm (1–1½in) cubes ripe pineapple
18 2.5–3.5cm (1–1½in) cubes ripe pawpaw, if available

Marinade
50g (2oz) butter
2 onions, finely chopped
1 clove garlic, finely chopped
2 ripe mangoes, peeled, stoned and mashed
1 teaspoon salt
2 tablespoons mild curry powder
½ teaspoon chilli pepper
2 tablespoons vinegar
1 tablespoon sugar

1 First prepare the marinade by heating the butter in a saucepan. Add the onion and garlic and fry until golden. Remove from the heat and stir in remaining marinade ingredients. Allow to cool.
2 Place the meat cubes in a large bowl, pour in the marinade and toss until the meat is well coated. Cover and refrigerate for 6–8 hours.
3 Thread the meat on to skewers alternating with pieces of fruit. Reserve the marinade. Grill the kebabs over charcoal for about 20 minutes or until the pork is cooked through, turning frequently.
4 When they are ready to serve heat the marinade in a small pan. Serve the kebabs with rice and the hot marinade.

Hirino souvlaki – Greek pork kebab

This is the most popular Greek kebab made of small pieces of pork and fat and eaten with a glass of ouzo and a Greek salad of fresh vegetables with feta cheese and black olives.

1kg (2lb) belly of pork

Marinade
juice 1 lemon
1 onion, finely chopped
1 clove garlic, finely chopped
3–4 bay leaves
150ml (¼ pint) white wine
4–6 tablespoons oil
2 teaspoons curry powder (optional)
¼ teaspoon turmeric

To serve
lemon wedges

1 Cut the meat into 2cm (¾in) pieces without removing the fat.
2 Mix all the marinade ingredients together in a large bowl, add the meat, mix well and leave for 5–6 hours.
3 Thread the meat on to skewers and cook over charcoal for

15–20 minutes, turning frequently so that the fat does not burn.

Serve with the lemon wedges.

The following are some variations on this basic recipe.

(A) Pork and pimento kebab

1kg (2lb) fillet of pork, cut into 2.5cm (1in) cubes
225g (8oz) pimentos, drained
175g (6oz) shallots
oil

Marinade
1 tablespoon finely chopped onion
2 tablespoons finely chopped parsley
½ teaspoon oregano
½ teaspoon coriander
½ teaspoon ginger
1 teaspoon salt
¼ teaspoon black pepper
¼ teaspoon chilli pepper

1 Combine all the marinade ingredients in a large bowl, add the meat, mix well and leave to marinate for about 4 hours.
2 Place the shallots in a bowl and cover with boiling water. Leave to stand for 2–3 minutes and then drain and peel. Cut the pimentos into 2.5cm (1in) squares.
3 Thread the meat, shallots and pimentos on to skewers and brush all over with oil. Grill over charcoal for about 20 minutes or until cooked through, turning and brushing with oil frequently.

Serve with a rice pilav.

(B) Pork with courgettes

1kg (2lb) pork fillet, cut into 2.5cm (1in) cubes
6 tomatoes
450g (1lb) courgettes, trimmed and cut into 2.5cm (1in) rings

Marinade
6 tablespoons oil
1 onion, finely chopped

2 teaspoons dried sage
1 teaspoon salt
½ teaspoon black pepper

1 Mix the marinade ingredients together in a large bowl,
add the meat and turn to coat well. Cover and refrigerate
for 6–8 hours, turning occasionally.
2 Thread the meat on to skewers with the courgette pieces
and tomatoes. Brush all over with the marinade and grill
over charcoal for about 20 minutes or until cooked through.
Brush frequently with the marinade.
  Serve with a plain rice pilav.

Goani kabab kari – Goanese-style kebab

There are many such recipes throughout the Indian sub-
continent where meat, usually lamb (though sometimes
pork as in this recipe from Goa) is grilled over charcoal, then
added to a curry sauce.
  This is a very spicy and hot kebab which, with a rice pilav,
some fresh vegetables and pickles will make a very tasty
meal.

1kg (2lb) pork, cut into 2.5–3.5cm (1in–1½in) cubes
thin slices fresh ginger

Curry sauce
3 tablespoons ghee or butter
2 onions, thinly sliced
3 cloves garlic, crushed
1 green pepper, thinly sliced
2 fresh chillies, seeded and thinly sliced
1 tablespoon cumin
1 tablespoon ground mustard seeds
1 teaspoon chilli pepper
2 teaspoons garam masala
1 teaspoon salt
½ teaspoon turmeric
60ml (2fl oz) malt vinegar
300ml (½ pint) water
3 tablespoons desiccated coconut

1 First prepare the sauce by melting the ghee or butter in a large saucepan. Add the onions and garlic and fry until soft. Add the peppers and all the spices, mix well and cook for one minute. Now add the remaining ingredients, stir well and simmer over a low heat.
2 Meanwhile thread the pork pieces on to skewers alternating with the slivers of ginger. Grill over charcoal for about 20 minutes, turning frequently.
3 When cooked slide the contents of the skewers into the sauce and simmer for a few more minutes until the sauce has thickened.

Serve on a bed of rice pilav.

Kharapak khorovadze – pork kebab with pomegranate syrup

This Armenian recipe from the Caucasus makes use of pomegranate syrup which adds a touch of unexpected piquancy.

1kg (2lb) boned leg of pork, cut into 3.5cm (1½in) cubes

Marinade
90ml (3fl oz) oil
1 large onion, finely chopped
1½ tablespoons chopped fresh oregano OR 1 tablespoon dried
  oregano
1 teaspoon salt
½ teaspoon black pepper
3 tablespoons pomegranate syrup (see page 255)

To serve
pomegranate syrup
fresh tarragon leaves, chopped (optional)

1 Mix the marinade ingredients together in a large bowl. Add the meat, toss to coat well, cover and refrigerate overnight.
2 Thread the pieces of meat on to skewers and grill over charcoal for 20–30 minutes or until cooked through, turning frequently.

3 Serve the kebabs sprinkled with the tarragon and
accompanied by a small bowl of pomegranate syrup into
which you dip each piece of meat.

Salorov khoz – pork kebab with prunes and quinces

A Caucasian pork kebab. If quinces are not available use
cooking apples instead.

1kg (2lb) lean pork, cut into 2.5cm (1in) cubes
24–30 prunes, stoned and soaked in water for 6 hours
6 quinces or cooking apples, peeled, cored and quartered

Marinade
5 tablespoons oil
1 teaspoon salt
½ teaspoon ginger
½ teaspoon turmeric
1 teaspoon sumac (see page 255)

1 Mix the marinade ingredients together in a large bowl,
add the meat and turn until well coated. Cover and
refrigerate for at least 2 hours.
2 Drain the prunes and thread the pork cubes and prunes
alternately on to skewers. Grill for about 20 minutes taking
care to ensure that the pork is cooked and that the prunes
are not burned.
3 While the kebabs are cooking heat the remaining
marinade in a pan, add the quartered quinces or apples and
simmer for 5 minutes. Drain.
4 Place the skewers on a large plate and arrange the quince
or apple quarters around the edge. Serve with pilav and
salad of your choice.

Dziranov khorovadze – pork kebab with apricots

Apricots and Armenia are like rice and China, for the world's
finest apricots originate in the land of Ararat. This
particular recipe, slightly adapted, hails from the Van region
and is best served with burghul pilav and a fresh mixed
salad.

1kg (2lb) fillet or boned leg of pork, cut into 2.5cm (1in) cubes
225g (8oz) whole dried apricots, halved and soaked overnight in
  300ml (½ pint) water
24 button mushrooms, wiped clean.

Sauce
1 tablespoon honey
2 tablespoons malt vinegar
1 teaspoon made mustard (English or American)
½ teaspoon salt
¼ teaspoon black pepper
¼ teaspoon cinnamon
¼ teaspoon sweet basil

Garnish
2 tablespoons chopped chives or tarragon

1 Drain the apricot halves and reserve the liquid. Thread
the pork on to skewers alternating with halved apricots and
mushrooms.
2 Make the sauce by placing the reserved liquid in a small
pan and stirring in the sauce ingredients. Bring to the boil
and simmer for 10 minutes.
3 Cook the kebabs over charcoal for about 20 minutes,
turning and brushing frequently with the sauce. This will
give the meat a fruity taste and a glazed finish. Serve on a
bed of burghul pilav accompanied by the apricot sauce.

Sheftalia – Greek pork sausage kebab

A classic kebab of Greek origin, but equally popular in
Cyprus and with Armenians. Caul fat (panna), which is the
outer covering of the paunch of the pig can be bought from
most butchers although you may have to give them a little
notice. In the Middle East it is sold by street vendors who
follow their mules from street to street offering, among
other things: sausage casings, lamb's heads, sweetbreads,
livers, kidneys, hearts etc.

  When panna is opened flat it has a patterned appearance of
fat on very fine tissue.

These kebabs make excellent appetizers, but they are often also served as a main dish with a rice pilav, salads and pickles.

450g (1lb) fatty pork, minced twice
450g (1lb) lamb or beef, minced three times
1 large onion, peeled and minced
4 tablespoons finely chopped parsley
2 teaspoons salt
½ teaspoon black pepper
225g (8oz) panna (pork caul fat)
warm water

1 In a large bowl mix the meats, onion, parsley, salt and pepper together and knead for about 3 minutes or until smooth.
2 Drop the panna into a bowl of warm water and leave for 2 minutes. Remove and carefully open, one at a time on a clean working top. Cut into 10cm (1in) squares using scissors or a very sharp knife.
3 Scoop out a spoonful of the meat mixture and shape it into a small sausage about 5cm (2in) long. Place near one edge of a piece of panna. Fold the edge and sides over and roll up firmly. Continue until you have used up all the mixture.
4 When all the sausages are made thread them on to flat skewers, 2–3 per skewer and grill over charcoal, turning frequently for about 10–12 minutes. The panna will slowly melt away keeping the sausages moist.

Bacon kebabs – bacon with mustard mayonnaise

A most attractive and unusual kebab. Serve with potatoes or a rice pilav and a salad of your choice.

225g (8oz) button mushrooms, wiped clean
2 tablespoons oil
12 rashers streaky bacon, rind removed
24 prunes, stoned. Use either drained tinned ones or dried ones
  soaked overnight
6 tomatoes, halved
12 gherkins

Mayonnaise
175g (6oz) cottage cheese
4 tablespoons mayonnaise
3 tablespoons single cream
1 teaspoon English mustard
½ teaspoon curry powder
¼ teaspoon chilli pepper

1 First prepare the mayonnaise by pressing the cheese through a sieve into a bowl with the back of a spoon. Add the remaining ingredients and mix thoroughly. Taste and adjust seasoning if necessary. Spoon into a serving bowl and refrigerate.
2 In a small bowl toss the mushrooms in the oil.
3 Stretch the rashers using the back of a knife and cut each in half crossways. Roll a bacon strip around each prune. Thread the rolls, halved tomatoes, mushrooms and gherkins on to skewers and brush with any remaining oil. Grill over charcoal for about 10 minutes, turning frequently until the bacon is golden. Serve immediately topped with the mustard mayonnaise.

Siew yok – spicy Malay pork kebab

This simple pork-pineapple recipe is best served with rice, although I have sometimes served it on its own as an appetizer.

You can increase the quantity of chilli pepper if you like – the Malays like their food fairly hot and make a clever use of hot and sweet combinations.

1kg (2lb) lean pork, cut into 2cm (¾in) cubes
1 large pineapple, peeled and cut into 2.5cm (1in) cubes
12 or more button mushrooms, wiped clean
12 or more small shallots

Marinade
150ml (¼ pint) soy sauce
2 tablespoons oil
2 cloves garlic, crushed
½ teaspoon chilli pepper – or more

¼ teaspoon cinnamon
¼ teaspoon ground cloves
½ teaspoon aniseed

1 Mix all the marinade ingredients together in a large bowl. Add the pork cubes, toss well, cover and refrigerate for at least 2 hours.
2 Ten minutes before cooking put the mushrooms in a bowl of warm water – this should prevent them splitting when skewering.
3 Thread the meat on to skewers alternating with pieces of pineapple, mushrooms and shallots. Grill over charcoal for 10–15 minutes, turning occasionally. Serve immediately.

Khozi tap-tap – pork with cracked wheat and sesame seed kebab

This recipe from Sis, in Cilician Armenia, makes an interesting use of minced pork with burghul and sesame seeds.
  Serve with yoghurt spooned over it and with pickles, salad and hot bread.

225g (8oz) burghul (cracked wheat)
450 (1lb) lean pork, minced
1 onion, very finely chopped
1 teaspoon oregano
2 teaspoons cumin
50g (2oz) sesame seeds
1 teaspoon salt
½ teaspoon allspice

To serve
300ml (½ pint) yoghurt
1 clove garlic, crushed
½ teaspoon chilli pepper

1 Soak the burghul in cold water for 10 minutes. Squeeze out excess water and place in a large bowl. Add the remaining ingredients. Keeping your hands damp knead the mixture for 8–10 minutes.

2 Divide the mixture into 12 portions. Dampen your hand and shape each portion along a skewer making a thin sausage about 15cm (6in) long. With finger and thumb press the centre of each kebab to divide it in two. Press the edges lightly to close around the skewer. Cook over charcoal for about 10 minutes, turning frequently to prevent burning.
3 Meanwhile in a small bowl mix the yoghurt, garlic and pepper.
4 When cooked arrange the tap-tap on a large dish, spoon the yoghurt mixture over the top and serve with pickles and salads.

Nem nuong – Vietnamese pork kebab

For this kebab the pork should be pounded with a mortar and pestle. To avoid this time-consuming process I suggest that you mince the meat twice.

In Vietnam a fish sauce 'nuoc mam' is used. This is a brown sauce which is the liquid of a small local fish. I have substituted soy sauce.

However there is no substitute for roasted ground rice and I suggest you make yours thus:

Put the ground rice in a small dry saucepan, set over a low heat and cook until lightly browned, stirring occasionally to prevent its burning.

Serve this kebab with rice or noodles and a salad of your choice.

1kg (2lb) pork fillet, minced twice
3 cloves garlic, crushed
1 teaspoon salt
1 tablespoon roasted ground rice
2 tablespoons saki or dry sherry
1½ teaspoons sugar
2 tablespoons soy sauce
3 tablespoons melted butter or ghee

Garnish
fresh sprigs mint or coriander
lemon wedges

Mix all the ingredients together in a large bowl and knead until well blended. Cover and set aside for 1 hour. Keeping your hands damp, take walnut-sized lumps of meat and form into sausages about 7.5–10cm (3–4in) long. Slide two sausages on to each skewer and squeeze tightly so that they do not move when the skewers are turned. Grill over charcoal for 10–15 minutes or until cooked through, turning frequently.

Serve with rice pilav or noodles and the recommended garnishes.

Poultry and
Game kebabs

The Greeks were the first to rear poultry as opposed to merely catching wild fowl, while the Romans went on to develop distinctive breeds. Basically poultry, which is often erroneously thought to refer only to the chicken, also includes turkey, duck, goose, pheasant, grouse, quail etc., i.e. any fowl which is bred specifically for the table.

The flavour of a bird depends on its age and, to a certain extent, on what it is fed. Generally the younger the bird the milder the flavour. Poultry meat is not only delicious, but is also healthy being a high source of protein, calcium, niacin, thiamine and riboflavin and low in calories.

Poultry nowadays comes free-range, frozen, ready-to-cook, in halves, quarters, pieces, deboned and rolled etc.

Chicken are excellent for roasting and grilling. They can also be stuffed with fruit, rice, herbs etc. Poussins, which are baby chickens (4–6 weeks old), have proportionally more meat on their bodies in relation to their weights, which is normally 450–550g (1–1¼lb). If a recipe requires the use of poussins then, unless otherwise stated allow one per person.

The most famous breed of duck is Aylesbury. It normally weighs 1.75–2.75kg (4–6lb) and is relatively fatty. Duckling, young duck usually weighs 1.5–1.75kg (3–4lb) and its breast is usually the meatiest part of the body. Although duck and duckling are not very popular in Britain they have enriched the French and Chinese cuisines with many a wonderful dish.

In Europe goose still dominates the festive scene while in America and Britain turkey has taken over as the Christmas and (in the U.S.), the Thanksgiving dinner. Turkey can vary greatly in weight, but the average is around 5–7kg (10–14lb). It is an excellent bird for roasting and grilling and should be cooked slowly so that the flesh does not dry out. Goose meat is dark in colour, tastes very sweet and is tender and moist.

There are other fowl, e.g. guinea fowl, capon, quail, woodcock, partridge, grouse, pheasant and pigeon, not forgetting teal, mallard etc. These, unfortunately, are not so easily available, are more seasonal and tend to be rather expensive. I have nevertheless included a few recipes mainly out of interest, but also because they do make excellent kebabs. If and when any of these birds are available do use them as they make a pleasant and tasty alternative to battery-produced chicken.

Rabbit can easily be purchased and though it is at its best stewed in casseroles it is still delicious when barbecued. It is available all the year round and has a flavour similar to that of chicken.

I have also included a recipe for venison. This can be bought from specialist shops. It is seasonal, from June to January and is expensive. The best meat is from the young male (buck); it is dark red and not fatty. The leg and saddle joints are best for grilling.

Grilled chicken

You can spit-roast at any one time as many chicken as the length of your spit and the width of your fire allows.

To spit-roast follow these simple steps:

1 Tie the wing tips over the breast and fasten the neck skin to the back with a skewer.

2 Push the spit through the bird from the tail end towards the front – the spit should emerge between the branches of the wishbone.

3 Tie the drumsticks and tail together.

4 Alternatively you can cut each chicken in half. If using a long spit then thread the chicken halves crossways onto the spit piercing each one through the thigh meat. If using individual skewers then push two skewers lengthways

through each half. This makes it easier to turn the chicken without it slipping around the skewer.

5 When cooking turn the chicken frequently brushing either with a baste or with any remaining marinade.

6 To test if the chicken is cooked pierce a thigh where the meat is thickest. If the juices run clear and not pink then the chicken is ready.

Chicken flesh absorbs the different flavours of marinades, bastes and sauces very well. The best results are, of course achieved when chicken is marinated for a time before cooking, but if your baste is tasty then you will also produce very satisfying and popular kebabs. If you are basting then do so frequently and warm any remaining baste at the end of the cooking time and either spoon it over the meat immediately before serving or pour it into a sauceboat alongside the kebabs.

The following are a few bastes and marinades that you may like to try when grilling chicken.

(A) A typical marinade from Turkey

150ml (¼ pint) oil
3 cloves garlic, crushed
juice 1 large lemon
1 teaspoon salt
½ teaspoon black pepper

1 Blend the ingredients in a large bowl, add the whole chicken or pieces and mix well. Leave at room temperature for at least two hours.

2 Thread the chicken on to spit or skewers and cook until tender using any remaining marinade as a baste.

(B) A brown sugar and tarragon vinegar marinade:

175g (6oz) brown sugar
150ml (¼ pint) tarragon vinegar
25g (1oz) butter

1 Put the ingredients in a small saucepan and heat gently until the sugar and butter have melted and the flavours are well blended. Pour into a bowl, add the chicken and mix well. Set aside at room temperature for at least 2 hours.
2 Thread the chicken on to spit or skewers and cook until tender using the remaining marinade as a baste while cooking.

(C) A herb baste:

75g (3oz) butter, melted
½ teaspoon savory
½ teaspoon rosemary
½ teaspoon thyme
½ teaspoon marjoram
½ teaspoon basil

1 Mix all the herbs together in a small bowl and stir in the melted butter.
2 Thread the chicken on to spit or skewers and brush the meat all over with the herb baste. Cook the chicken, brushing frequently with the baste.

(D) Redcurrant baste:

1 × 350g (12oz) jar redcurrant jelly
2 tablespoons lemon juice
1 tablespoon Worcestershire sauce
1 teaspoon allspice
1 teaspoon salt
¼ teaspoon black pepper

1 Put all the ingredients in a small saucepan and gently bring to the boil. Thread the chicken on to spit or skewers and cook until tender, basting frequently.

(E) Ranch baste:

150ml (¼ pint) cider vinegar (malt vinegar will also do)
90ml (3 fl oz) oil
1 tablespoon Worcestershire sauce

½ onion, finely chopped
1 teaspoon salt
1 tablespoon tomato purée
1 teaspoon tabasco
25g (1oz) butter, melted

1 Although this is a recipe for a baste there is enough of it
to use as a marinade if you would like to leave the chicken
in it for an hour or two before cooking to allow the meat to
absorb the extra flavour. Mix all the ingredients in a bowl.
If marinating the chicken then place it in the bowl and turn
to coat thoroughly. Set aside for 1–2 hours.
2 Thread the chicken on to spit or skewers and cook until
tender, turning and basting frequently.

(F) A honey-lime marinade from the Caribbean

300ml (½ pint) fresh orange juice
3 tablespooons fresh lime juice
4 tablespoons chopped parsley
1 tablespoon dry mustard
1 clove garlic, crushed
4 tablespoons soy sauce
4 tablespoons honey
50g (2oz) butter, melted
1 teaspoon salt

1 Mix all the ingredients together in a large bowl, add the
chicken, stir well and leave at room temperature for about
2 hours.
2 Thread the chicken on to spit or skewers and cook until
tender, turning and basting frequently with marinade.
3 Heat any remaining marinade and serve with the kebabs.

(G) Mechoui baste from Morocco

1 tablespoon paprika
1 teaspoon cumin
½ teaspoon chilli pepper
1 teaspoon salt
75g (3oz) butter, melted

1 Mix all the ingredients together and use to baste chicken frequently while cooking.

(H) Mustard baste:

This is a very tasty baste to use on drumsticks. It is enough for 6–8.

1 tablespoon ready mixed English mustard
25g (1oz) butter, melted
juice ½ lemon
1 teaspoon chopped chives
1 teaspoon salt
½ teaspoon black pepper

1 Mix all the ingredients together and use to brush the drumsticks thoroughly. Set aside for 15–20 minutes.
2 Cook over charcoal, basting frequently.

Chicken stuffing If you wish to stuff the chicken do so from the neck end and do not pack it in too tightly as it will swell during cooking.

For recipes for stuffing see *Stuffed turkey*, but use only half the quantities given.

Murg tikka – skewered chicken with yoghurt and ginger

This is an easy and delicious way to cook chicken and is a 'must' on the menu of most Indian restaurants.

It is traditionally served with an onion and tomato salad and chapattis.

6 chicken breasts, about 225g (8oz) each

Marinade
1 onion, roughly chopped
1 clove garlic, sliced
2.5cm (1in) piece ginger, peeled and chopped
3 tablespoons lemon juice
1 teaspoon coriander
1 teaspoon cumin
5 tablespoons yoghurt

Garnish
1 tablespoon raisins
2 dried red chillies, chopped
1 teaspoon salt
2 tablespoons fresh coriander or mint leaves, chopped

1 Bone and skin the chicken breasts. Cut the meat into 2.5cm
(1in) pieces.
2 Place the onion, garlic and ginger in a blender and blend
until smooth. Scrape the paste into a small bowl and stir in
the lemon juice. Mix the spices and yoghurt together in a
large bowl and stir in the onion paste. Add the chicken
pieces, mix thoroughly and leave to marinate for 2–3 hours
at room temperature or cover and refrigerate overnight.
3 Thread the chicken pieces on to skewers and cook over
charcoal for 10–12 minutes or until cooked, turning
frequently.
4 Serve immediately on a bed of pilav with the garnish
ingredients mixed together and sprinkled over the top.

Tandoori murg – tandoori chicken

This is a North Indian dish made famous throughout the
world in the last few years by the countless tandoori
restaurants.

Traditionally the chicken is cooked in a Tandoor (similar to
the Turkish 'Tendor' and the Armenian 'Tonir') which is a
cylindrical clay oven still popular in the remote villages of
the Caucasus, Iran and Turkey as well as India.

In a modern kitchen tandoori chicken can be cooked in the
oven, but it is extremely suitable, indeed as good as the real
thing, to cook it over a charcoal fire.

1 × 1.75–2.5kg (4–5lb) chicken, skinned
1 teaspoon salt
1 teaspoon cayenne pepper
½ teaspoon black pepper
2 tablespoons lemon juice

Marinade
7.5cm (3in) piece ginger, peeled and chopped
4 cloves garlic, crushed

2 teaspoons whole coriander seeds
2 tablespoons lemon juice
1 tablespoon ground cumin
5 tablespoons yoghurt
1 tablespoon cayenne pepper
1 teaspoon red vegetable colouring
3 tablespoons melted ghee or butter

1 In a small bowl mix together the salt, cayenne and black
peppers and the lemon juice and rub all over the chicken. Set
aside for about 1 hour.
2 Meanwhile, to prepare the marinade, mix all the
ingredients together in a large bowl. After the hour place
the chicken in the bowl, coat it generously with the marinade,
cover and refrigerate for 12–18 hours.
3 Remove the chicken from the marinade and thread whole
on to a spit or two large skewers. Tie the wings together
and tie the legs to the tail end. If you like you can cut the
chicken in half and place on an oiled grill.

Cook over charcoal, turning and basting frequently with the
marinade so that the chicken does not burn. A spit-roasted
whole chicken will take about 1–1½ hours to cook through.
4 Serve on a large platter garnished with thinly sliced onions
and tomatoes and chopped chilli peppers dressed with lemon
juice. Accompany with chapatti or nan bread (pages 205,
206).

Saté pendang ayam – Malaysian chicken kebab

In Malaysia and in adjoining South-east Asian countries
coconut milk is used a great deal. Here it is part of the
marinade and gives an added richness. The chicken is first
simmered in coconut milk and spices then grilled until
tender.

Serve with a rice pilav or with bread.

6 chicken quarters

Sauce
25 blanched almonds
2 green chillies
3 cloves garlic

grated rind 1 lemon
juice 1 lemon
2 teaspoons turmeric
1 tablespoon coriander seeds
½ teaspoon chilli pepper
1 teaspoon sugar
1 teaspoon salt
3 tablespoons oil
300ml (½ pint) coconut milk. This can be bought tinned or you can
  prepare it by mixing 75g (3oz) creamed coconut with 300ml (½
  pint) water

1 Place the almonds, chillies, garlic, lemon rind and juice,
turmeric, coriander seeds, chilli pepper, sugar and salt into
a blender and blend to a paste. Heat the oil in a large
saucepan, add the paste and fry gently for 3–5 minutes,
stirring frequently. Stir in the coconut milk and add the
chicken quarters. When the mixture comes to the boil, lower
the heat, cover the pan and simmer for 15–20 minutes.
2 Remove the chicken pieces from the pan and thread on to
flat skewers. Grill over charcoal, basting with the mixture
in the pan occasionally, for about 15–20 minutes or until
tender.
3 Meanwhile continue to simmer the sauce until it thickens.
4 When the chicken is cooked and golden serve with a rice
pilav and spoon some of the spice mixture over the top.

Kebab me ouftim yayim – Israeli chicken in wine

This is an Israeli kebab adapted from a Greek kebab called
Stithos Kotas Skoaras which, a Cypriot friend assures me,
is as old as the legend of Venus and the vineyards on the
slopes of the Troodos mountains.
  Israeli or not, it makes a clever use of avocado – a local
speciality – as an accompaniment and it does taste excellent.

6 chicken breasts, skinned and boned

Marinade
2 green peppers, each cut into 6 pieces
2 onions, each cut into 6 wedges

6 large mushrooms, wiped clean
3 sticks celery, each cut into 4 pieces
juice 4 lemons
150ml (¼ pint) oil
150ml (¼ pint) dry red wine
2 cloves garlic, finely chopped
2 bay leaves
1 teaspoon coriander
1 teaspoon salt
½ teaspoon black pepper

To serve
3 avocados
50g (2oz) sugar
1 tablespoon lemon juice
150ml (¼ pint) red wine

Garnish
fresh mint leaves

1 Mix all the marinade ingredients together in a large bowl.
Add the chicken breasts, turn to coat well, cover and
refrigerate overnight.
2 Remove the breasts from the marinade and thread on to
skewers. Thread the vegetables on to skewers. Brush the
chicken and vegetables with the marinade and grill over
charcoal for 12–15 minutes, turning and basting frequently.
3 While the kebabs are cooking cut the avocados in half and
remove the stones.
4 Mix the sugar, lemon juice and wine together in a small
bowl and then pour into the halved avocados. Garnish with
the mint leaves and serve with the kebabs.

Sis khorovou – chicken marinated in sumac and
pomegranate juice

This dish from Sis – the capital of Cilician Armenia – has a
fascinating mixture of ingredients, including pomegranates
and pine kernels. Serve with a burghul (cracked wheat) pilav.

6 chicken portions
50g (2oz) pine kernels, use split almonds if these are not available

Marinade
2 large ripe pomegranates
1 clove garlic, crushed
1 teaspoon sumac (see page 255)
1 teaspoon salt
4 tablespoons oil
2 spring onions, finely chopped

Garnish
watercress
2 tablespoons chopped parsley or chives

1 Cut the pomegranates in half and empty the seeds into a small saucepan. Add the garlic, sumac, salt, oil and spring onions. Cook gently for 10 minutes, stirring frequently. Allow to cool.
2 Place the chicken pieces into a shallow bowl and pour in the marinade. Turn the pieces so that they are well coated and then leave to marinate at room temperature for 2–3 hours.
3 Thread the chicken pieces on to skewers and grill for 15–20 minutes, turning and basting frequently with the marinade.
4 Five minutes before serving, heat any remaining marinade in a small pan and stir in the pine kernels or almonds.
5 Serve the chicken pieces on a bed of burghul pilav (page 200) with the hot marinade poured over the top. Garnish with the watercress and parsley or chives.

Chicken Saigon

A chicken kebab, marinated in lemon juice, from Vietnam. I suppose this ought now to be called Ho-Chi-Minh City kebab!

It is traditionally served on a bed of rice with the kebabs laid diagonally and liberally strewn with julienne of lemon.

Raeta (page 212) is a fine accompaniment, as is jajig (page 212).

1 × 1.75–2kg (3½–5lb) chicken
4 lemons
1 clove garlic, crushed

1 teaspoon salt
½ teaspoon turmeric
1 large green pepper, cut into 3.5cm (1½in) squares
1 large red pepper, cut into 3.5cm (1½in) squares
1 onion, quartered and separated into layers
50g (2oz) butter, melted
1 teaspoon grated nutmeg

1 Joint the chicken, skin and bone the joints and cut the
flesh into 3.5cm (1½in) pices.
2 Peel the rind from the lemons as thinly as possible and
then cut it into fine julienne (strips). Blanch in boiling water
for 1 minute, drain and set aside.
3 Squeeze the lemons and pour the juice into a large bowl.
Stir in the garlic, salt and turmeric. Add the pieces of
chicken, mix well and leave at room temperature for one
hour.
4 Thread the chicken pieces on to skewers, alternating with
the pepper and onion pieces. Brush the kebabs with the
melted butter and dust with the grated nutmeg. Grill for
12–15 minutes, turning frequently.

Pollo alla diavolo – chicken with herb kebab

A well-known Italian dish of grilled chicken with herbs. It is
quick to prepare, and thus ideal if you are in a hurry.

6 chicken quarters
2 large cloves garlic, halved
1 teaspoon salt
½ teaspoon black pepper

Baste
100g (4oz) butter
2 tablespoons oil
juice ½ lemon
1 tablespoon chopped parsley
1 tablespoon chopped fresh basil OR 1½ tablespoons dried basil

1 Rub the chicken quarters all over with the garlic and then
sprinkle with the salt and pepper. Set the chicken aside.
2 Heat the butter and oil in a small saucepan. Remove from

the heat and stir in the lemon juice and herbs. Brush the chicken pieces all over with this mixture and grill over charcoal for 15–20 minutes, turning and basting frequently.
3 When cooked transfer the chicken to a serving dish and pour over any remaining warmed butter-herb mixture.

Yakitori – chicken kebab with teriyaki sauce

This is the most popular chicken kebab in Japan, widely found in both restaurants and street corner cafés.

Authentically, the kebabs are brushed and basted with the teriyaki sauce and then cooked over charcoal.

12 chicken livers, each one cut into 3 pieces
1 × 1.5kg (3lb) chicken
18 shallots, peeled
1 large green pepper, cut into 2.5cm (1in) squares

Marinade
3 tablespoons saké (Japanese rice wine; see page 255)
4 teaspoons soy sauce (try to use the Japanese one, but the Chinese is equally good)
1½ teaspoons sugar
2.5cm (1in) piece ginger, peeled and grated OR ½ teaspoon ground ginger

Teriyaki sauce
120ml (4fl oz) mirin (page 255)
120ml (4fl oz) soy sauce
120ml (4fl oz) chicken stock

1 Skin and bone the chicken and cut the flesh into pieces the size of the liver pieces.
2 Put the marinade ingredients into a large bowl, add the liver and chicken pieces and mix well. Cover and refrigerate for several hours.
3 Blanch the whole shallots in boiling water for 2 minutes, then drain.
4 Remove the meat from the bowl and reserve the marinade. Thread the meat on to skewers, alternating the shallots and pepper pieces.

5 Make the teriyaki sauce by putting all the ingredients in a saucepan. Add the reserved marinade, bring to the boil, simmer for 2 minutes, then remove from the heat. Brush the kebabs with the sauce and cook, turning and basting frequently with the sauce, for 8–10 minutes or until cooked through and golden.

6 Serve immediately with boiled rice and the sauce.

Kabab-e-joojeh – Iranian chicken kebab

A famed Iranian kebab that is always accompanied by chelo rice (page 195), a pat of butter and sumac.

3 × 1kg (2lb) chickens, each cut into 8 pieces – 2 breasts, 2 wings, 2 drumsticks and 2 thighs
50g (2oz) melted butter
small pinch ground saffron *OR* saffron strands dissolved in 3 teaspoons water

Marinade
1 onion, finely chopped
6 tablespoons lemon juice
1½ teaspoons salt
¼ teaspoon nutmeg
¼ teaspoon cinnamon

1 Mix the marinade ingredients together in a large bowl. Add the chicken pieces and turn until well coated. Cover and refrigerate overnight.

2 Thread the pieces on to 6 skewers each containing 1 breast, 1 wing, 1 drumstick and 1 thigh.

3 Mix the melted butter and saffron water and stir into the remaining marinade. Brush the kebabs all over with this mixture and grill for 8–10 minutes, turning and basting occasionally.

4 Serve the kebabs with chelo rice. Place a pat of butter on top of the rice and sprinkle liberally with sumac. As the butter melts mix the rice up so that the butter and sumac are distributed evenly throughout the rice.

Kai yang – chicken kebab with coriander and garlic

This chicken kebab comes from Thailand, a land famed for her rice dishes and imaginative use of spices. This dish makes clever use of garlic and pepper. Serve on a bed of boiled rice with a simple sliced tomato and onion salad.

6 chicken breasts, boned and halved. Do not remove the skin.

Marinade
6 cloves garlic
2 teaspoons salt
2 tablespoons black peppercorns
3 whole plants of fresh coriander, washed thoroughly
2 tablespoons lemon juice

1 Crush the garlic and salt in a mortar and pestle. Scrape the paste into a bowl. Crush the peppercorns coarsely in the mortar and pestle and add to the garlic paste.
2 Chop the coriander plants finely – including the stems, leaves and roots. Add to the garlic mixture and mix well. Add the chicken pieces and rub the mixture in well. Set aside at room temperature for 2–3 hours or cover and refrigerate overnight.
3 Either thread the chicken pieces on to skewers or lay on an oiled grill and cook for about 10 minutes, turning frequently until the skin is crisp and the meat tender.
 Serve immediately with boiled rice and a salad.

Ajam panggang pedis – spicy Indonesian chicken kebab

From Indonesia this is a recipe for grilled chicken with hot spices. It is somewhat similar to the saté dishes.
 Serve with a plain rice pilav or a cooked vegetable dish of your choice.

6 chicken quarters, skin and flesh scored to help flavours penetrate

Marinade
2 teaspoons black pepper
2 teaspoons salt
2 teaspoons chilli pepper
3 tablespoons finely chopped onion

2 cloves garlic, finely chopped
3 tablespoons soy sauce
1 tablespoon brown sugar
2 tablespoons lemon juice
2 tablespoons peanut oil OR vegetable oil

1 Mix all the marinade ingredients together in a large bowl.
Add the chicken pieces and rub the marinade into them
thoroughly. Set aside at room temperature for 2–3 hours or
cover and refrigerate for several hours.
2 Either thread the pieces on to skewers or lay on an oiled
grill and cook over charcoal. Cook for about 10 minute. or
until tender, turning and basting frequently. Serve
immediately.

Saté ajam ajawa – Javanese kebab

From the island of Java comes this marinated chicken kebab
rich in ingredients yet subtle in aroma and taste.
  Serve with kuah saté 2 (see page 250).

6 chicken breasts, skinned, boned and flesh cut into 2.5cm (1in)
  cubes

Marinade
1 onion, finely chopped
2 cloves garlic, crushed
2 teaspoons white pepper
1 teaspoon salt
2 tablespoons brown sugar
150ml (¼ pint) soy sauce

1 Mix all the marinade ingredients together thoroughly in
a large bowl. Add the chicken cubes and stir to coat with
the marinade. Set aside at room temperature for 2–4 hours,
turning occasionally.
2 Thread the chicken on to skewers and grill over charcoal
for 8–10 minutes or until cooked through, turning and
basting frequently with the marinade.
3 Serve garnished with fresh salad vegetables and
accompanied with Kuah Saté 2.

Chicken with chutney apples

An American dish that gives the chicken pieces a beautiful golden appearance. Serve with a rice pilav or potatoes and chutney apples – see recipe below.

6 chicken legs, each cut into thigh and drumstick

Marinade
1 large onion, finely chopped
1 clove garlic, finely chopped
1 tablespoon French mustard
2 tablespoons Worcestershire sauce
150ml (¼ pint) apple juice
150ml (¼ pint) oil
2 tablespoons honey or golden syrup

To serve
6 large apples
6 tablespoons chopped chutney of your choice

1 Mix all the marinade ingredients together in a large bowl until well blended. Add the chicken pieces, turn so that all the joints are well coated, cover and refrigerate for several hours.
2 Place the pieces on an oiled grill and cook over charcoal for 15–20 minutes, turning occasionally until cooked through and golden.
3 When the chicken pieces are on the grill, prepare the apples. Core them and remove 2.5cm (1in) peel from the stem end. Fill each centre with 1 tablespoon chutney. Wrap each apple in foil and place around the edge of the fire. Turn them a few times while cooking.
4 Serve the chicken joints on a large platter garnished with the apples.

Maryland kebabs – chicken and banana kebabs

I have included this recipe for the very simple reason that I love it. It has an unusual but very tasty combination of chicken, banana, bacon, onions and peppers.
  Serve with potatoes or a pilav of your choice.

6 chicken breasts, skinned, boned and flesh cut into 2.5cm (1in)
  pieces
3 bananas, peeled and cut into 4 pieces
6 rashers streaky bacon, rind removed
2 large green peppers, cut into 3.5cm (1½in) squares
12 baby onions, peeled
9 bay leaves, halved

Marinade
1 tablespoon honey
150ml (¼ pint) hot water
2 tablespoons lemon juice
½ teaspoon salt

1 Place the marinade ingredients in a shallow dish and stir
until the honey has dissolved. Add the chicken pieces, turn
to coat well and then set aside at room temperature for 2–3
hours.
2 When ready to cook remove the chicken pieces and reserve
the marinade.
3 Cut each bacon rasher in half crossways. Wrap each piece
of banana in a piece of bacon. Thread the chicken, banana-
bacon rolls, peppers, onions and halved bay leaves alternately
on to skewers. Grill over charcoal for 8–10 minutes, turning
and basting regularly with the marinade.
  Serve immediately.

Brochettes Amalfi – chicken liver and kidney kebab

A popular dish with an intriguing combination of chicken
livers, kidneys and ham.
  Serve with potatoes and a fresh vegetable salad.

25g (1oz) butter
750g (1½lb) chicken livers
450g (1lb) lamb's kidneys, trimmed of fat, skin and gristle and
  halved
450g (1lb) cooked ham, cut into 2.5cm (1in) cubes
6 medium onions, quartered
2 green peppers, cut into 2.5cm (1in) squares
50g (2oz) melted butter

1 Melt the 25g (1oz) butter in a frying pan. Add the chicken livers and fry over a moderate heat for 2–3 minutes. Remove with a slotted spoon, drain on kitchen paper and leave to cool.

2 Thread alternate pieces of chicken liver, kidneys, ham, onion quarters and green pepper on to skewers. Using a pastry brush coat the brochettes with melted butter. Grill over charcoal for about 8–10 minutes, turning and basting frequently with melted butter.

3 Serve immediately with potatoes and a salad.

The Pilgrim Fathers were the first to discover the wild turkey – ancestor of the present domestic bird.

When guinea fowl were first introduced into England and Europe they were generally known as turkey-cocks because they were brought by 'Turkey merchants' engaged in the spice trade with the Middle East; also, perhaps, because of their red feathers which are like the tassel the Turks used to wear on their fezzes. The turkey has, in a few hundred years, become the festive bird of wedding and Christmas dinners and, in America, of Thanksgiving.

It is at its best roasted and is very suitable for stuffing.

Below is a typical description for turkey on a spit, followed by several marinades and bastes.

Spit-roast turkey

1 Rinse the turkey inside and out and dry with kitchen paper.

2 Rub the cavity with salt OR with the baste you have chosen.

3 Insert the spit rod into the centre of the neck skin, run it through the body cavity parallel to the backbone. Bring the spit rod out just above the tail. Insert the spit fork into the breast and the other fork into the tail.

4 Use string to tie the wings close to the body and the legs and tail together.

5 It is difficult to give exact cooking times. In general allow about 20 minutes per 450g (1lb) and 20 minutes extra. However make sure that the bird is cooked through by inserting a fork into a thigh. If the juices run clear it is cooked.

6 Baste the bird frequently.

Marinades and bastes

(A)

150ml (¼ pint) soy sauce

4 tablespoons honey

90ml (3fl oz) sherry

5cm (2in) piece fresh ginger, peeled and finely chopped

3 cloves garlic, finely chopped

Mix all the ingredients together in a large bowl and marinate the turkey overnight in the refrigerator, turning the bird occasionally.

(B)

90ml (3fl oz) dry white wine

50g (2oz) butter, melted

1 clove garlic, finely chopped

1 teaspoon rosemary

1½ teaspoons salt

½ teaspoon black pepper

Combine all the ingredients together in a large bowl and marinate the turkey in it for several hours, turning occasionally.

(C)

50g (2oz) butter, melted

1 teaspoon rosemary

1 teaspoon oregano

2 teaspoons sumac (see page 255)

Mix these ingredients together in a small bowl and use to baste the turkey frequently while it is cooking.

(D)

90ml (3fl oz) oil

90ml (3fl oz) lemon juice

2 cloves garlic, finely chopped

1 tablespoon finely chopped fresh mint
1 teaspoon salt
1 teaspoon coarsely ground black pepper

Mix the ingredients together in a large bowl, add the turkey, turn to coat with the marinade and refrigerate for several hours, turning the bird occasionally.

(E)
This marinade is sufficient for 6 turkey drumsticks

150ml (¼ pint) dry red wine
90ml (3fl oz) oil
1 teaspoon oregano
1 clove garlic, finely chopped
1½ teaspoons chilli pepper
1½ teaspoons salt
2 tablespoons sugar
150ml (¼ pint) soured cream

Combine all the ingredients except the soured cream in a large bowl. Add the drumsticks, turn to coat and set aside for 2–3 hours.

Grill the drumsticks over charcoal, basting frequently with the marinade.

Blend 4 tablespoons of the marinade with the soured cream and heat, but do not boil, the sauce in a small pan. Serve the sauce with the drumsticks.

Stuffings

The stuffings below are as suitable for chicken as for turkey, but remember to halve the quantities if stuffing a chicken.

(A)
Veal forcemeat stuffing – used to stuff the neck end
75g (3oz) fresh breadcrumbs
25g (1oz) butter, melted
1 small onion, finely chopped
175g (6oz) veal, minced
75g (3oz) lean bacon minced
1 egg, lightly beaten

1 teaspoon salt
½ teaspoon black pepper

Place all the ingredients in a large bowl and mix well.
Gradually add sufficient water to bind the stuffing.

(B)
Sausage stuffing – used to fill the body cavity
750g (1½lb) pork sausagemeat
100g (4oz) fresh breadcrumbs
2 shallots, chopped
100g (4oz) belly pork, finely chopped
1 egg
salt and pepper to taste

Place all the ingredients in a large bowl and knead until well
blended. Pack loosely into the body cavity.

(C)
Chestnut stuffing – usually used to stuff the neck end, though there
may be sufficient for the body cavity depending on the size of the
bird.
1 portion veal forcemeat stuffing – see recipe above
2 tablespoons chopped parsley
50g (2oz) streaky bacon, rind and gristle removed
175g (6oz) chestnut purée
grated rind 1 lemon

Prepare veal forcemeat stuffing and mix in the parsley. Chop
bacon finely and fry gently in a pan for 2–3 minutes. Mix
drained bacon into stuffing together with the chestnut purée
and lemon rind.

Khentzorov hentgahav – turkey with apples

This fragrant, subtle recipe comes from Lori in Armenia. It
is best served with a simple saffron rice pilav and a plate
of tomatoes, cucumbers, radishes, lettuce, olives and other
salad vegetables. This recipe will serve 8.

one × 3.5kg (8lb) turkey
2 tablespoons salt
75g (3oz) melted butter

8 cooking apples – exact amount depends on number of people being
  served. Allow 1 per person
50g (2 oz) sugar
cinnamon
300ml (½ pint) water

Garnish
parsley and mint sprigs

1 Wash and dry the bird inside and out. Rub the salt into
the skin with your fingers and rub a little butter into the
cavity.
2 Insert the spit rod through the turkey and tie the string
around it to hold the wings close to the body. Tie the legs
and tail together.
3 Brush with the melted butter and cook over charcoal,
turning and basting regularly. Grill for 2–2½ hours. Test
if it is cooked by piercing a thigh with a fork – if the juices
run clear it is cooked. While roasting collect 3–4 tablespoons
of the dripping in a pan placed under the turkey.
4 Meanwhile, 40 minutes before the end of the cooking time,
peel and core the apples. Pour the dripping into a large
shallow dish and stand the apples in it. Sprinkle them with
the sugar and a good pinch of cinnamon. Add as much of
the water as possible without the apples floating. Cook in a
moderate oven, basting with the liquid occasionally for
about 30 minutes or until the apples are just tender.
5 Serve the turkey on a bed of saffron rice on a large platter
surrounded by the apples, garnished with sprigs of parsley
and mint and with the liquid from the apple pan spooned
over the turkey.

Chiboot me hodoo – turkey kebab

This is a recipe from Israel.
  Turkey makes an excellent kebab, especially when served
with salads, pickles and chutneys.

1kg (2lb) boned turkey breast, cut into 2.5–3.5cm (1in–1½in) cubes
1 large onion, layers separated and cut into 2.5cm (1in) squares
2 large green peppers, cut into 2.5cm (1in) squares

Marinade
150ml (¼ pint) oil
juice 1 large lemon
1 clove garlic, crushed
1 bay leaf, crushed
1 teaspoon oregano
1 teaspoon salt
½ teaspoon white pepper

1 Mix the marinade ingredients together in a large bowl.
Add the cubed meat, toss well, cover and refrigerate for 24
hours, turning occasionally.
2 Thread the meat on to skewers, alternating with pieces of
onion and pepper. Grill over charcoal for 8–10 minutes,
turning and basting frequently with the remaining
marinade. When the meat is just cooked but still moist
remove from the fire and serve immediately with a kasha
(page 202) or burghul pilav (page 200) plus pickles and salads.

Kabab-e-boughalamu – turkey and prawn kebab

This recipe from Southern Iran makes use of the unusually
tasty prawns of the Indian Ocean.
  The yoghurt marinade makes the meat very soft and gives
a tangy flavour. You can use chicken breasts instead of
turkey if you wish.
  Serve with pilav and salad.

1kg (2lb) turkey breast, skinned, boned and cut into 2.5–3.5cm
  (1in–1½in) pieces
2 large green peppers, cut into 3.5cm (1½in) squares
350g (12oz) large prawns, peeled
18–24 button mushrooms, wiped clean

Marinade
150ml (¼ pint) yoghurt
2 tablespoons lemon juice
1 clove garlic, crushed
½ teaspoon salt
¼ teaspoon black pepper
1 teaspoon paprika
1 tablespoon finely chopped parsley

1 Mix all the marinade ingredients together in a shallow
dish. Add the turkey and pepper pieces and the prawns,
gently turn to coat with the marinade and then set aside at
room temperature for one hour.
2 Thread the turkey, pepper, prawns and the mushrooms on
to skewers and brush with any remaining marinade. Cook
over charcoal for 8–10 minutes or until just cooked through,
turning and basting frequently. Serve immediately with a
salad and pilav of your choice.

Duck on a spit

Attach the bird to the spit in the normal way (see Grilled
chicken page 129) and cook for 1½–2 hours, turning and
basting frequently.

Below are some tasty marinades and bastes.

Orange baste

150ml (¼ pint) orange juice
60ml (2fl oz) soy sauce
1 teaspoon honey
¼ teaspoon black pepper

Mix the marinade in a large bowl, add the duck and turn
until well coated. Set aside at room temperature for 3–4
hours, turning occasionally. Remove the bird from the
marinade, spit it and cook, basting frequently with any
remaining marinade.

Mustard baste

1½ teaspoons dry mustard
2 teaspoons Worcestershire sauce
2 teaspoons grated orange peel
1 teaspoon grated lemon peel
3 tablespoons olive oil
2 tablespoons malt vinegar

Mix all the ingredients together in a small bowl and use to
baste the bird while it is cooking.

Herb marinade

150ml (¼ pint) oil
60ml (2fl oz) lemon juice
1 teaspoon salt
1 teaspoon marjoram
1 teaspoon thyme
¼ teaspoon black pepper
2 tablespoons chopped chives
½ teaspoon basil
½ teaspoon cinnamon
1 clove garlic, crushed

Mix all the ingredients together in a large bowl. Add the duck and turn to ensure it is well coated. Set aside at room temperature for 3–4 hours. Remove bird from the marinade, spit it and cook, turning and basting frequently with the remaining marinade.

Yoghurt marinade

300ml (½ pint) yoghurt
1 clove garlic, crushed
1 teaspoon ground ginger
1 teaspoon chilli pepper
½ teaspoon cinnamon
1 teaspoon salt
4 bay leaves, crushed

Mix all the ingredients together in a large bowl. Add the duck and turn until well coated. Set aside at room temperature for 3–4 hours.

Remove the duck from the marinade and cook, turning and basting frequently with the remaining marinade.

Hawaiian duck on a spit

This dish, from the Hawaiian island of Mani, although of Chinese origin is popular all over the islands.

one 1.75–2.75kg (4–6lb) duck, washed and dried

Marinade
300ml (½ pint) soy sauce
1 clove garlic, crushed
2 tablespoons sugar
½ teaspoon allspice
½ teaspoon chilli pepper

Garnish
fresh pineapple rings

1 Mix all the marinade ingredients in a large bowl. Add the
duck and turn to coat well. Set aside at room temperature
for 3–4 hours.
2 Remove the bird, attach to the spit and cook for 1½–2
hours, turning and basting frequently.
 Serve with a plain pilav and garnished with the pineapple
rings.

Dindings duck – duck marinated in spices

This duck kebab from Malaysia is ideal for a small dinner
party

one 1.75kg –2.75kg (4–6lb) duck, cut into 6 serving pieces

Marinade
1 tablespoon ground coriander
2 teaspoons ground fenugreek
2 teaspoons ground cumin
¼ teaspoon ground cloves
¼ teaspoon ground nutmeg
1 teaspoon ground black pepper
1 teaspoon salt
½ teaspoon tabasco
juice 1 lemon
1 onion, finely chopped
2 cloves garlic, finely chopped
1cm (½in) piece fresh ginger, peeled and finely chopped
50g (2oz) desiccated coconut soaked in 75ml (2½fl oz) boiling water

1 Mix all the marinade ingredients together in a large bowl
until they form a thick paste. Add the duck pieces and rub

the paste all over them. Set aside at room temperature for
3–4 hours, turning occasionally.
2 Thread the duck pieces on to flat skewers or lay on an oiled
grill and cook over charcoal for 20–30 minutes, turning and
brushing occasionally with any remaining marinade. Test if
the bird is cooked by inserting the point of a sharp knife
into a thigh. If the juices run clear then the duck is cooked.
3 Serve with a plain pilav, jajig (page 212) and vegetables
and/or salads of your choice.

Goose

'De less you meddles wid 'em, de better dey be' – Advice on cooking
geese

Goose is best at its simplest.
  It is more fatty than chicken and therefore does not need to
be brushed with melted butter when cooking.

Crisp-roast goose

one 2.75–3.75kg (6–9lb) goose, washed and dried
1 lemon, halved
salt

1 Rub the goose inside and out with the lemon halves. Rub
salt over the inside and out. Attach to a spit (see Grilled
chicken page 129) and grill over charcoal, turning regularly
for 2–2½ hours or until it is fork-tender and the skin is crisp.
2 Serve immediately with apple sauce (page 253). Other
traditional accompaniments are bread sauce, potatoes or a
pilav and vegetables.

Gaasestag med aebler og svedsker – goose with apple and prune stuffing

This is an adaptation of a Danish favourite – in fact it is the
traditional Christmas Eve dinner in Denmark.
  As with all stuffed recipes this is also excellent when cooked

in the oven, but grilling it over charcoal does, I believe, give the meat an extra flavour. Serve on a bed of rice with sultanas or nuts and a fresh salad.

one 2.75–3.75kg (6–9lb) goose with giblets
900ml (1½ pints) water
1 lemon, halved
salt and pepper
225g (½lb) stoned prunes, soaked in a little water for 2 hours
450g (1lb) apples, peeled, cored and coarsely chopped

Sauce
1 tablespoon cornflour
1 tablespoon redcurrant jelly

1 Put the giblets in a saucepan with the water and a pinch of salt and bring to the boil. Lower the heat and simmer for 2 hours or until the liquid is reduced by half. Drain and reserve the stock.
2 Rub the inside and out of the goose with the cut lemon and sprinkle with some salt and pepper.
3 Drain the prunes and chop them coarsely. Mix with the chopped apples and put into the body cavity of the goose. Sew up the opening.
4 Attach the bird firmly to a spit (see Grilled chicken p 129) and roast over charcoal for about 2½–3 hours, turning regularly.
5 To make the sauce, collect some of the drippings from the goose in a small saucepan and stir in the cornflour. Gradually mix in the giblet stock to make a thick gravy. Add the redcurrant jelly and heat until it has melted.
6 Remove the goose from the spit and lay on a large platter, perhaps on a pilav of your choice. Remove the trussings and serve with the redcurrant sauce.

Judi kebab – poussin kebab

This famous Armenian kebab makes excellent use of a lemon and olive oil marinade liberally spiced with garlic.
Use poussins about 450g (1lb) in weight and serve with a fresh salad and lavash bread.

6 poussins, washed and dried

Marinade
150ml (¼ pint) olive oil
2 cloves garlic, crushed
1 large lemon, thinly sliced
1 tablespoon sumac (see page 255)
2 teaspoons salt
1 teaspoon black pepper

Sauce
1 clove garlic, crushed
juice 1 lemon
4 tablespoons olive oil
½ teaspoon cumin

1 Cut each poussin into 8 pieces, i.e. 2 breasts, 2 wings, 2 drumsticks and 2 thighs. Remove the skin from each piece.
2 Mix all the marinade ingredients together in a large bowl. Add the chicken pieces, turn to coat and then cover and refrigerate for at least 8 hours or overnight.
3 Thread the chicken on to flat skewers arranging the pieces so that each skewer holds the 8 pieces of one poussin. Cook over charcoal, turning and basting frequently with the remaining marinade for about 10 minutes. When cooked slide the kebabs off the skewers on to a large serving plate.
4 Mix the sauce ingredients together and sprinkle it over the chicken immediately before setting.

Assafeer and hamam meshwi – skewered birds and pigeons

These recipes are for small birds and pigeons. I have included them more as a curiosity than anything else. This is because, although small birds, e.g. sparrow, thrush and lark are most suitable, in Britain and America the killing and eating of these birds is not only illegal but also extremely distasteful to most people. However, in most Middle Eastern countries as well as North Africa, Asia and South America *Assafeer* – small birds – are highly prized and extremely popular.

As a curiosity, therefore – and only that:

1 Pluck and remove entrails. Wash thoroughly and dry.
2 Cut off beak and lower legs.
3 Rub salt and pepper all over the body.
4 Thread the birds on to skewers and grill over charcoal for about 6–8 minutes.
5 Squeeze a few drops of lemon juice over each bird and eat – bones and all!

The result is marvellous and perhaps when you happen to be passing through the Orient you may pluck up your courage and try!

As for *hamam* – this is pigeon.

The pigeons in Britain are not quite up to the standard of those of the Middle East and so you could try poussin instead.

1 Prepare as above.
2 Thread on to skewers and grill over charcoal for 10–12 minutes or until cooked through.
3 Serve with lemon juice and chopped parsley sprinkled over the top and accompanied by a fresh salad.

Pigeons can be marinated very successfully. The following marinades are sufficient for 6 pigeons.

(A) An Egyptian marinade

150ml (¼ pint) oil
2 teaspoons cumin
2 teaspoons coriander
juice 1 large lemon OR 1 onion, finely chopped
2 cloves garlic, finely chopped
1 teaspoon chilli pepper

Mix all the ingredients together in a large bowl. Add the birds, turn to coat and set aside for 2 hours. Grill over charcoal, turning and basting frequently.

(B) A Syrian marinade

150ml (¼ pint) oil
juice 1 large lemon
1 teaspoon salt
½ teaspoon black pepper
2 bay leaves, crushed

Mix all the ingredients together in a large bowl, add the
birds and set aside for 2 hours. Grill over charcoal, turning
and basting frequently. Serve sprinkled with chopped chervil
or parsley.

(C) A Caribbean marinade

150ml (¼ pint) oil
1 teaspoon salt
½ teaspoon black pepper
2 tablespoons chopped chives
2 tablespoons chopped parsley

Garnish
Black butter, i.e. 75g (3oz) butter with black pepper

1 Mix the marinade ingredients in a large bowl, add the
birds, turn to coat and set aside for 2 hours.
2 While the pigeons are marinating melt the butter in a
small pan and continue heating gently until it turns dark
brown. Season it to taste with freshly ground black pepper
and place in the refrigerator to harden.
3 Thread the birds on to skewers and grill over charcoal,
turning and basting occasionally.
4 While they are cooking shape the butter into 6 pats. Serve
each bird with a pat of butter on it and garnished with lime
wedges.

Gooung kui – Korean pheasant kebab

'In spring the pheasant calls out his whereabouts' – Korean proverb

This recipe incorporates many of the basic ingredients of the
Korean cuisine.
  Usually the pheasants in this dish are cooked in a small

amount of oil, but here I have adapted the dish to be grilled over charcoal.

3 pheasants, cleaned, washed and halved

Marinade
150ml (¼ pint) soy sauce
150ml (¼ pint) tahina (see page 255)
1 teaspoon ground black pepper
4 spring onions, chopped – including the green tops
2 cloves garlic, finely chopped
3 teaspoons brown sugar
3 teaspoons oil

1 Mix all the marinade ingredients together in a large bowl. Place the halved pheasants in the bowl, turn to coat and set aside at room temperature for about 2 hours.
2 Thread each half on to two skewers – this will make it easier to turn the birds. When all the halves are thus threaded, cook over charcoal for about 15–20 minutes, turning and basting frequently.
3 Heat the remaining marinade.
4 Serve the pheasants on a large platter on a bed of boiled rice and pour the marinade over the top.

Kabab-e-gharghavol – Iranian pheasant kebab

If you are lucky enough to come by some pheasants then try this very pleasant Iranian kebab.

3 pheasants, quartered

Marinade
6 tablespoons oil
3 tablespoons lemon juice
1 teaspoon turmeric
1 teaspoon salt
½ teaspoon paprika

1 Mix the marinade ingredients together in a large bowl, add the pheasant pieces, mix well and leave to marinate at room temperature for at least 2 hours.
2 Thread the pheasant pieces on to skewers and cook,

turning and basting frequently for 15–20 minutes or until cooked through.
3 Serve on a bed of saffron rice and accompany with a yoghurt and cucumber salad.

NB In England pheasant can only be shot between October 1 and January 31. The best are killed in November and December. The cock and hen may be sold singly or as a brace. The hen is usually considered the tastiest and will serve 3 people while a cock should serve 4.

Pheasant stuffed with nuts

A Middle Eastern dish which is now popular far beyond its original boundaries. One of the favourites of Ottoman sultans and Persian shahs it is, even today, rather expensive.

3 young pheasants – hung (note that the pheasants should be hung, i.e. 'aged', either well wrapped for 4 days in the refrigerator OR for 2–3 days at room temperature).

Stuffing
225g (8oz) nuts – a mixture of pistachios, walnuts and cashews, finely chopped
600ml (1 pint) chicken stock
6 slices bacon, grilled and chopped
100g (4oz) butter
450g (1lb) lamb or chicken liver, finely chopped
225g (8oz) raisins
1 teaspoon salt
½ teaspoon chilli pepper

Garnish
2 large ripe pomegranates, split and seeded

1 Carefully clean the pheasants, wash thoroughly, dry and set aside.
2 Prepare the stuffing by placing the chopped nuts and chicken stock in a saucepan. Bring to the boil, lower the heat and simmer until the nuts are tender and most of the liquid has been absorbed. Mix in the bacon.
3 Melt half the butter in a small pan, add the chopped liver

and fry for a few minutes. Add the contents of this pan and the raisins to the nut mixture and season with the salt and chilli pepper.

4 Stuff the pheasants with this mixture and truss them.

5 Thread the pheasants on to a large spit and grill over charcoal for about 45–60 minutes or until tender, turning frequently and basting with the remaining butter which you have melted.

6 Serve on a large platter garnished with the pomegranate seeds.

'Rabettes flesh is best of all wylde beestes, for it is temperate and doth nourish and is syngularly prized of Physiche' – A Boorde

Khorovadz nabasdag – grilled rabbit

The finest rabbit for grilling over an open fire is a young rabbit which is white-fleshed like a chicken and is treated as such. Fat old rabbits are not suitable – although they make excellent stews and pies!

This Armenian recipe, also known as 'Hunter's Rabbit' is for a whole rabbit grilled over an open fire and is best served with a rice pilav and sautéed apples and quinces.

two young rabbits, skinned, drawn and with liver reserved
6–8 cloves
4 cloves garlic, halved lengthways
50g (2oz) butter
2 cloves garlic, finely chopped
150ml (¼ pint) red wine
juice 1 lemon
salt and pepper to taste

Marinade
300ml (½ pint) red wine
150ml (¼ pint) oil
2 bay leaves, crushed
1 teaspoon mint
3 tablespoons finely chopped parsley

1 Wash and dry the rabbits. With the point of a sharp knife make incisions in the bodies and stud the rabbits with cloves and pieces of garlic.

2 Mix the marinade ingredients together in a large bowl. Add the rabbits and turn to coat well. Cover and refrigerate for 12–18 hours, turning occasionally.

3 Remove the rabbits from the marinade and thread onto a spit or large skewers. Grill over charcoal for 1–1½ hours or until cooked, turning regularly.

4 Meanwhile melt the butter in a small pan. Chop the reserved liver finely and add to the pan together with the chopped garlic. Remove from the heat, leave to cool for 5 minutes and then pound to a smooth paste with a mortar and pestle. Return the paste to the saucepan and gradually stir in the wine, the lemon juice and salt and pepper to taste. Bring to the boil, lower the heat and simmer for 10 minutes, stirring constantly.

5 When cooked remove the rabbits from the fire and serve on a large plate on a bed of rice, accompanied by the sauce.

Kabab khargoush – Iranian-style rabbit kebab

This is a highly appreciated delicacy in the East. When the meat is grilled over charcoal it is very tasty and succulent.

You can use hare instead of rabbit if you wish.

Serve with fresh salads or vegetables of your choice and bread.

1kg (2lb) boneless rabbit meat, cut into 3.5cm (1½in) pieces
1½ teaspoons salt
½ teaspoon black pepper
1 teaspoon cumin
1 teaspoon garam masala
oil for basting

Garnish
fresh tarragon, mint, parsley and chives
1 onion, thinly sliced

tomatoes, cucumbers, radishes etc, sliced
lemon wedges
1 tablespoon sumac powder (p. 255)

1 Mix the spices together in a small bowl and then rub this
mixture thoroughly into the pieces of meat. Thread them
on to skewers and grill over charcoal for 10–15 minutes,
turning and basting frequently with oil.
2 When cooked arrange the skewers in the centre of a large
serving dish and garnish with the fresh herbs and
vegetables. Sprinkle the kebabs with the sumac and serve
with bread.

Umbles grill – venison kebab

Also known as 'Hunter's Grill' this is a very simple venison
kebab from England – a medieval recipe adapted to our
modern taste. Venison is a very dry meat and so bacon fat is
used with it.
  Ideal accompaniments are roast potatoes and redcurrant or
gooseberry jelly.

1kg (2lb) venison, from the top of the leg, cut into 2.5cm (1in) pieces
300ml (½ pint) cider
1 teaspoon black pepper
18–24 button mushrooms, wiped clean
bacon fat, cut into small pieces
18–24 shallots
50g (2oz) melted butter

1 Pour the cider into a large bowl and stir in the black
pepper. Add the venison pieces and the mushrooms, mix
well and set aside to marinate at room temperature for about
4 hours.
2 Thread the meat, mushrooms, bacon fat and shallots
alternately on to skewers. Grill over charcoal for about 30
minutes or until cooked, turning and brushing frequently
with melted butter.
3 Serve on a large platter with roast potatoes and
accompanied by some redcurrant or gooseberry jelly.

Fish kebabs

To lie and to eat fish needs care. – Spanish saying

Fish has always been an important source of protein for man. Since there are thousands of species in the seas and lakes and several hundreds of these are consumed by us in ever growing quantities, it would be impossible to include all the different dishes and their recipes, but in reality you will find that any one recipe will suit a great many different types of fish. A few of the recipes may include fish unfamiliar to you. This is because the warm waters of the Mediterranean and Caribbean contain a much greater variety of fish than the colder waters further north. However, today we are not so limited in variety or so dependent on our own natural supply because of the widespread use of refrigeration and the growing number of fish farms in large reservoirs or artificial lakes.

Fish naturally come in many different shapes and sizes. It is possible, and indeed preferable to cook some whole, while others are more suited to being treated in small pieces. There are four basic cuts of fish – round fish fillet, flat fish fillet, steak and cutlet. As fish dries out very quickly when cooked over a charcoal fire, do not buy thin fillets.

Buying

1. Look for firm, even-textured flesh, clear shiny eyes, bright gills and a clean smell.
2. Avoid fish with a blue or green tinge as it will not be fresh. Remember that more food poisoning is caused by old or second-rate fish than any other food.

Cleaning

1 To scale – cover a wooden board with newspaper and, holding the fish by the tail scrape away the scales from the tail towards the head using the blunt edge of a knife.
2 To clean – slit the fish along the belly from behind the gills to just above the tail. Scrape out and discard the entrails.
3 Rinse the fish thoroughly under cold running water.
4 With a pinch of salt rub away any black skin that may be inside the cavity.
5 The head and tail can be left on if desired. If you wish to remove them, cut the head off just below the gills and slice off the tail. Also cut off the fins and gills.

Cooking

In some seaside restaurants and on picnics fish can be cleaned, washed and cooked straight from the water with just a little oil or melted butter brushed over them and sprinkled with a pinch of salt. This is the easiest and most economical way of cooking fish, but marinating it does enhance the flavour considerably.

 A special point to note is that it is not easy to cook fish on a spit or skewer unless it is cut into small pieces as with e.g. skewered swordfish, Trabazon eel kebab, Machchi kebab etc. This is because it flakes easily when it cooks and therefore tends to break up so a minimum of handling is essential. There are two main methods of grilling fish over an open fire, both of which achieve very satisfactory results
1 *Double Grill* – The two parts are hinged together and fold over to hold the fish in place. The grill should be slightly oiled before placing the fish in it as this prevents the fish from sticking to it. Do not put the fish directly over the hottest part of the fire or the flesh will dry out before it is cooked. The flesh should be soft and juicy and the skin crisp and brown. To help achieve this it is always wise to baste the fish frequently. The simplest baste is melted butter flavoured with a little lemon juice.

These grills are now readily available from the 'barbecue' section of most department and hardware stores.

2 *Cooking in foil* – I, personally, do not like this method although it does produce a succulent and often tasty result. The point is that a kebab should be cooked over charcoal. Grilling by electric or gas, or using a foil wrap is not really producing a genuine kebab as the whole essence of the kebab is the wonderful aroma and flavour that it absorbs from the charcoal. Cooking in foil, or for that matter in a banana leaf as they do in the Caribbean, does not provide this. It merely cooks the fish.

However, if you cannot obtain a double grill then by all means use foil – making sure that you use the tasty marinades suggested in some of our recipes.

Shellfish

These make very tasty kebabs, providing you remove their shells first! In general they require very little cooking.

Fish kebabs, because of their distinctive flavour require very light sauces and fairly plain accompaniments – not forgetting a bottle of cold white wine!

Barbecued fish

Fish is excellent grilled, either whole, in steaks or in fillets.

Most fish lend themselves to this type of cooking and so it would be tedious and irrelevant to list them. Therefore I have included below a simple recipe for a fish kebab, then added several different marinades – all suitable for most varieties of fish.

As fish flakes when it cooks it is usually advisable to cook larger pieces in an oiled double grill as this makes it much easier to turn without breaking.

1kg (2lb) fish. If small allow 1 per person, otherwise cut into steaks.

Marinade
5 tablespoons oil
1 teaspoon oregano
salt and pepper to taste

To serve
2 tablespoons chopped parsley
Hunter's orange (see page 246)

1 Clean and wash the fish and pat dry with kitchen paper.
2 Mix the oil, oregano, salt and pepper together in a shallow dish. Add the fish and turn to coat well with the marinade. Set aside for about 2 hours.
3 Place the fish in a lightly oiled double grill and cook over charcoal, turning and basting frequently with the remaining marinade. Cooking time will depend on the thickness of the fish, but you can test it with a fork. If the fish flakes easily then it is cooked.
4 Transfer fish to a large serving plate, sprinkle with the parsley and spoon the lemon sauce over it.

The following are a few different marinades you might like to try instead of the one above.

Wine marinade

150ml (¼ pint) dry white wine
4 tablespoons olive oil
2 cloves garlic, crushed
2 teaspoons rosemary
2 teaspoons marjoram
½ teaspoon black pepper

Mix all the ingredients together, add the fish and leave to marinate for about 2 hours.

Butter marinade

75g (3oz) butter, melted
juice 1 lemon
½ teaspoon coriander
1 teaspoon salt
½ teaspoon black pepper

Mix all the ingredients together, add the fish, turn to coat well and leave to marinate for about two hours.

Soy-ginger marinade

2 tablespoons oil
5 tablespoons soy sauce
2 tablespoons honey OR 3 tablespoons brown sugar
2 tablespoons wine vinegar
1 level tablespoon grated fresh ginger
1 clove garlic, crushed

Mix all the ingredients together in a large bowl. Add the fish and turn to coat well. Leave to marinate for 3–4 hours.

Tzook narinchov – orange-flavoured fish kebab

This is an adaptation of a famed Armenian dish where the subtle and rather unusual combination of fish and orange creates a tasty and visually appealing result.

6 white fish steaks, each about 225g (8oz) in weight and 1cm (½in) thick

Marinade
150ml (¼ pint) oil
1 clove garlic, crushed
1 teaspoon salt
3 bay leaves
grated rind of 2 oranges

Sauce
90ml (3 fl oz) oil
juice 1 large lemon
juice 2 large oranges
pinch salt

Garnish
2 oranges, peeled, white pith discarded, thinly sliced into rings
1 onion, sliced crossways and pushed out into rings
about 20 black olives
sprigs of fresh mint

1 Wash the fish and dry on kitchen paper.
2 Mix the marinade ingredients together in a shallow dish. Add the fish and turn to coat well. Set aside for 2–4 hours.
3 Place the fish in a lightly oiled double grill and cook for

8–10 minutes, turning every few minutes to prevent burning.
4 Meanwhile prepare the sauce by mixing all the ingredients
in a small bowl.
5 When the fish is cooked arrange the slices on a serving
dish. Surround with the orange slices and scatter the onion
rings, olives and fresh mint over the top. Spoon the sauce
evenly over the fish and orange slices.

Stuffed whole fish

Many fish taste excellent when stuffed. Ideally it should be
cooked in the oven or under the grill in a pan, but with a
slight adjustment there is no reason why it cannot be
charcoal grilled so that the aroma and flavour of the
charcoal is also added to the taste.

Below are a few suggestions for fish stuffings. Remember
that fish sizes vary considerably so you may have to adjust
the amount of stuffing you make a little. The first stuffing
below is sufficient for a 3.5kg (8lb) fish, e.g. tuna, salmon,
pike or river trout. It should be sufficient for 8–10 people.

3.5kg (8lb) whole fish, cleaned, washed and dried
salt and pepper.

Baste
oil
75g (3oz) butter, melted
juice 2 lemons

Stuffing
50g (2oz) butter
1 onion, finely chopped
225g (8oz) dry breadcrumbs
100g (4oz) grated carrot
100g (4oz) mushrooms, finely sliced
2 tablespoons finely chopped parsley
juice 1 lemon
1 egg
1 clove garlic, crushed
2 teaspoons salt
1 teaspoon marjoram
½ teaspoon black pepper

1 Rub the cavity of the fish with a little salt and pepper.
2 Prepare the stuffing by melting the butter in a saucepan,
adding the onion and frying until soft but not brown. Add
all the remaining ingredients and cook gently for 5–8
minutes and then use it to stuff the fish. Close the opening
by threading with string. Brush the skin with a little oil and
place in a large double grill.
3 Mix the butter and lemon juice together. Cook the fish over
charcoal for about 30–45 minutes, turning and brushing very
frequently with the butter-lemon juice mixture.
4 Serve the fish on a large platter. Remove the string and
cut the fish into portions. Garnish with lemon wedges and
chopped parsley if you wish.

The stuffing below is sufficient for a fish about 2.5kg (5lb)
in weight which will feed 5–6 people.

Stuffing
350g (12oz) cooked plain rice
150ml (¼ pint) salad dressing (oil, lemon juice, garlic, salt and
  pepper)
1 tin (approx 125g/5oz) water chestnuts, halved
50g (2oz) spring onions, chopped
1 green pepper, thinly sliced
1 teaspoon salt
½ teaspoon black pepper
½ teaspoon oregano

Baste
50g (2oz) melted butter

Mix all the stuffing ingredients together and fill the fish
cavity. Sew up and cook as in the recipe above, basting with
the melted butter.

Below is a stuffing sufficient for 6 individual fish, e.g. trout

Stuffing
175g (6oz) walnuts, very finely chopped or coarsely ground
3 tablespoons lemon juice
3 tablespoons finely chopped parsley
1 egg, beaten
2 tablespoons oil
1 teaspoon salt

Mix all the stuffing ingredients together in a bowl and then stuff each fish with some of the nut mixture. Close each opening with cotton thread. Brush the fish with oil and place in a double grill. Grill over charcoal for about 15 minutes turning frequently.

Serve with lemon wedges.

Gan saengsun – Korean fish kebab

Koreans have some excellent fish dishes and this grilled fish is one of them. It is simple yet has a very subtle flavour. Serve on a bed of rice pilav.

6 whole fish OR 6 large fillets, about 225g (8oz) each

Marinade
3 tablespoons soy sauce
1 teaspoon sugar
3 tablespoons prepared sesame seeds (see Cho kan jang, steps 1 and 2, on page 244)
1½ tablespoons tahina (see page 255)
1 clove garlic, finely chopped
1 teaspoon grated fresh ginger

1 Clean wash and dry the fish.
2 Mix all the marinade ingredients together in a shallow dish. Add the fish and turn to coat thoroughly. Set aside for about 30 minutes, turning occasionally.
3 Place the fish in a lightly oiled double grill and cook over charcoal for 8–10 minutes or until the flesh is tender and the skin is crisp. Brush frequently with the marinade.

Serve on a bed of rice.

Tzook kounjutov – fish and sesame seeds kebab

An absolutely delightful fish recipe from Armenia making use of sesame seeds and tahina sauce.

The traditional accompaniment is a platter of fresh vegetables and herbs.

6 halibut fillets, 225g–275g (8–10oz) each, washed and dried

150ml (¼ pint) soured cream
100g (4oz) toasted sesame seeds

Marinade
4 tablespoons pomegranate syrup (p. 255)
2 teaspoons lemon juice
1 teaspoon salt
½ teaspoon black pepper

To serve
300ml (½ pint) tahinijeh (see p. 251)

1 Mix the marinade ingredients together in a shallow dish.
Add the fish fillets, turn to coat well and set aside for 15
minutes.
2 Empty the soured cream into a shallow dish. Spread the
toasted sesame seeds over a large plate.
3 Remove one fillet from the marinade and, with a pastry
brush, coat both sides with soured cream. Then lay each
side in the sesame seeds to coat thoroughly. Place in an oiled
double grill. Repeat with remaining fillets.
4 Grill over charcoal for 10–15 minutes, turning
occasionally.
5 Meanwhile prepare the tahina sauce.
6 When the fish is cooked serve with fresh vegetables and
herbs, lavash or pita bread (pages 207, 208) and with the
tahina sauce, which is used as a dip.

Tzook garmrook – spicy fish kebab

This very simple recipe from Cilician Armenia was a
favourite of my father who liked hot spicy dishes. The hot
sauce is similar to a famed Syrian sauce called Muhamara.
  The only things I can possibly recommend as
accompaniments are a burghul pilav and a glass of cold beer
to quench your thirst.

1kg (2lb) tuna, mackerel, hake or snapper

Marinade
5 tablespoons olive oil
4 tablespoons lemon juice

1 clove garlic, crushed
1 teaspoon salt
½ teaspoon black pepper
½ teaspoon coriander

Garmrook sauce
4 tablespoons olive oil
100g (4oz) breadcrumbs
1 chilli pepper, very finely chopped, including seeds
4 tablespoons lemon juice
1 tablespoon paprika
175g (6oz) walnuts, coarsely chopped
1 teaspoon salt

Garnish
2 tablespoons finely chopped parsley
2 tablespoons pine kernels

1 If the fish are small, e.g. mackerel, allow 1 per person, otherwise cut into steaks. Wash, clean and dry on kitchen paper.
2 Mix the marinade ingredients together in a shallow dish. Add the fish, turn to coat well, cover and refrigerate for several hours or overnight.
3 Remove the fish and place in an oiled double grill. Grill over charcoal for 10–15 minutes, turning and basting with the remaining marinade frequently.
4 Meanwhile prepare the garmrook sauce by mixing all the ingredients together thoroughly in a bowl. If the oil is not enough add just sufficient to make a very light paste. Pour this into a large platter. Remove the fish from the grill and arrange over the sauce. Garnish with the parsley and pine kernels and serve immediately with a burghul pilav.

Kinome yaki – Japanese fish kebab

This dish is typical of Japanese cooking in its simplicity. Serve as a luncheon or supper dish on a bed of plain rice and with a simple green salad.

6 large herrings or mackerel, slit open and cleaned out

Marinade
6 tablespoons sweet saké (*mirin*) or dry sherry
6 tablespoons saké
6 tablespoons soy sauce
1 tablespoon sugar
2.5cm (1in) piece fresh ginger, peeled and chopped

Garnish
1 teaspoon freshly ground black pepper

1 Rinse the fish inside and out and dry with kitchen paper. Place one on a board with the cavity side down and the flaps of the skin spread out. Press the backbone firmly with the heel of your hand until the fish is flattened. Turn the fish over and carefully remove the backbone and the large bones near the head. Discard the bones and cut the fish in two lengthways. Make three cuts on the skin side, but do not cut completely through the flesh. Repeat these processes with the remaining fish.
2 In a small saucepan heat the sweet saké and the saké over a moderate heat for 3 minutes. Ignite the wines, remove the pan from the heat and allow to burn until the flames die down. Stir the soy sauce, sugar and ginger into the wines and then pour the marinade into a shallow dish. Cool, then place the fish fillets in the dish and baste well with the liquid.
3 Transfer the fillets to an oiled grill and cook for 5 minutes. Baste with the liquid, turn and cook for a further 5 minutes.
4 Place the cooked fillets on a serving dish and sprinkle with the black pepper. Pour the basting liquid into a sauceboat and serve with boiled rice.

Malu kabab – Sri Lankan fish kebab

Sri Lanka, off the southern tip of India has some beautiful dishes, in particular curries of prawns and other fish.

This spicy recipe from Jaffna, in the north of the island, has a rich marinade of exotic spices.

Serve this dish with a rice pilav as well as chutneys, pickles and a bowl of fresh salad.

1kg (2lb) fish fillets, washed and dried

Marinade
2 tablespoons lemon juice
1 teaspoon salt
1 teaspoon turmeric
1 onion, thinly sliced
2 cloves garlic, crushed
3 slices fresh ginger
¼ teaspoon cinnamon
¼ teaspoon ground cloves
1 tablespoon coriander
1 teaspoon cumin
½ teaspoon chilli pepper
½ teaspoon black pepper
3 tablespoons oil
90ml (3fl oz) water

1 Mix all the marinade ingredients together in a large bowl.
Add the fish fillets, turn to coat thoroughly and then cover
and refrigerate for 2 hours.
2 Remove the fillets and place in an oiled double grill. Cook
over charcoal for about 10 minutes, turning occasionally.
3 Meanwhile warm the marinade in a small pan.
4 Serve the fish with a rice pilav and accompanied by the
hot marinade as a sauce.

Machchi kebab – Indian fish kebab

This fish kebab from India comes marinated in many regional
spices. It was traditionally cooked in a tandoor, but is
excellent over a charcoal fire. Serve it with chapattis or pita
bread and a salad of thinly sliced onions, chopped green chillies
and mint leaves dressed with lime juice.

1kg (2lb) fish fillets, cut into 2.5cm (1in) cubes

Marinade
2 teaspoons finely chopped fresh ginger
2 cloves garlic, finely chopped
1 teaspoon salt
1 teaspoon garam masala
juice 2 lemons

300 ml (½ pint) yoghurt
1 teaspoon chilli pepper
3 teaspoons coriander
2 tablespoons plain flour

1 Put all the marinade ingredients in a large bowl and mix thoroughly. Add the fish cubes, toss well and set aside for 30 minutes at room temperature.
2 Thread the cubes onto skewers and cook over charcoal for 8–10 minutes, turning frequently. Remove from the fire and serve immediately.

Kiliç şiş – swordfish kebab

This famed swordfish kebab, popular in all the seaside restaurants of Istanbul, has the fish grilled with bay leaves which give the flesh a wonderful flavour. It is traditionally served with a plain rice pilav and Tarator sauce – see p. 249.

1kg (2lb) swordfish, skinned, boned and flesh cut into 2.5cm (1in)
  cubes
1 onion, cut crossways into ½cm (¼in) slices and pushed out into
  rings
3 tablespoons lemon juice
2 tablespoons olive oil
1½ teaspoons salt
½ teaspoon black pepper
20–30 large bay leaves

Garnish
chopped parsley

1 Mix the onion, 1½ tablespoons of the lemon juice, 1 tablespoon of the oil, the salt and pepper. Add the fish and toss thoroughly. Leave to marinate for 2–3 hours at room temperature OR 4–5 hours in the refrigerator.
2 Meanwhile soak the bay leaves for one hour in boiling water and then drain.
3 Remove the fish from the marinade and thread on to skewers alternating each piece with a bay leaf. Press firmly together so that the flavour passes from the leaves to the fish. Mix the remaining oil and lemon juice together and

use to baste the kebabs while they are cooking. Grill over charcoal for 8–10 minutes or until the fish is golden.

Serve off the skewers on a bed of rice pilav and with some tarator sauce.

Psari skharas – fish kebab marinated in oregano and brandy

Here is an extravagant dish from Greece where fish is found in abundance and is relatively cheap.

I recommend this kebab for its wealth, its absolutely dazzling appearance and for what I can only call its 'Mediterranean' taste.

Serve with a plain pilav and fresh vegetables.

4 fillets of sole, cut into small pieces
450g (1lb) prawns, shelled and deveined
12 large clams
12 oysters
12 mushrooms caps, wiped clean
1 green pepper, quartered and then each quarter halved
2 red peppers, quartered and then each quarter halved.

Marinade
1 tablespoon oregano
juice 1 large lemon
1 teaspoon salt
½ teaspoon black pepper
150ml (¼ pint) brandy

To serve
lemon wedges
brandy

1 Mix all the marinade ingredients together in a large bowl. Add all the prepared fish, turn to coat thoroughly and then leave to marinate at room temperature for about two hours.
2 Meanwhile put the mushrooms in warm water to soften a little.
3 Remove the fish pieces from the marinade and thread them on to skewers alternating with pieces of pepper and the

mushrooms. Grill over charcoal for 5–8 minutes, turning
frequently.
4 Arrange the skewers on a large platter and garnish with
the lemon wedges. Pour a little more brandy over the fish
and ignite. Serve immediately while still flaming.

Trabazon eel kebabi – Eel kebab

This fine Turkish dish is a speciality from the Black Sea
region and is best eaten with a plain rice pilav and fresh
vegetables.

1kg (2lb) conger eel, skinned and filleted, washed and cut into 2.5cm
  (1in) pieces
1 teaspoon salt
1 teaspoon black pepper
6 thick slices bread, crusts removed, cut into 2.5cm (1in) cubes
12 small tomatoes, halved
6 bay leaves
4 tablespoons olive oil

Garnish
lemon wedges
fresh tarragon and spring onions

1 Rub the salt and pepper into the eel cubes. Thread the eel,
bread cubes and tomato halves alternately on to 6 skewers
placing a bay leaf in the centre of each skewer. Brush the
kebabs with the oil. Grill over charcoal for about 8–10
minutes or until the eel is tender and the bread toasted. Turn
and brush frequently with the oil.
2 Serve immediately on a bed of rice pilav with the lemon
wedges and a side dish of fresh tarragon and spring onions.

L'Hootz mischui – mackerel and vegetable kebab

An unusual and tempting way of serving fish from North
Africa where the fish is marinated, cooked on skewers and
served on a bed of cous-cous.

6 mackerel, cleaned, gutted and with backbones removed
6 shallots

6 small tomatoes
6 button mushrooms, wiped clean
1 large green pepper, cut into 2.5cm (1in) squares

Marinade
60ml (2fl oz) white wine vinegar
60ml (2fl oz) olive oil
½ teaspoon salt
¼ teaspoon cumin

To serve
Cous-cous (see p. 201)

1 Cut each mackerel into four slices. Thread these on to skewers, alternating with the shallots, tomatoes, mushrooms and green pepper.
2 Mix the marinade ingredients together in a large shallow dish. Lay the prepared skewers in the dish, turning once or twice and leave to marinate at room temperature for about two hours, turning occasionally.
3 Remove the kebabs from the dish and cook over charcoal for 10–15 minutes, turning and basting frequently with the remaining marinade. When the flesh of the fish flakes easily it is cooked.
4 Serve the kebabs laid on a bed of cous-cous rice.

Hawaiian fish kebab

This speciality of the island of Hawaii makes use of the local pineapple crop and contrasts it with chilli pepper to make a very exciting taste.

6 large white-fleshed fish fillets, washed and dried
1 small ripe pineapple – peeled and cut into rings. You can use
  tinned pineapple rings if you wish.

Marinade
25g (1oz) butter
1 onion, finely chopped
1 tablespoon soy suace
1 tablespoon vinegar
1 teaspoon honey
2 tablespoons tomato purée

½ teaspoon curry powder
½ teaspoon turmeric
juice 1 lemon
½ teaspoon chilli pepper
1 teaspoon salt
150ml (¼ pint) pineapple juice

1 To prepare the marinade, heat the butter in a small
saucepan. Add the onion and fry for several minutes until
it has softened. Stir in all the remaining ingredients and
simmer over a low heat for about 10 minutes. Remove from
the heat and leave to cool.
2 Arrange the fillets in a large shallow dish and pour the
cooled marinade over them, spreading it out with a pastry
brush. Set aside for about one hour.
3 Arrange the fillets on an oiled double grill and cook over
charcoal for 10–15 minutes, turning once or twice until
cooked, but not dry.
4 Arrange on a platter and garnish with the pineapple rings.

Ikan pangank – Indonesian fish kebab

One of my personal favourites. This fish kebab, marinated in
coconut milk and spices, hails from Indonesia. Coconut milk
is, of course very popular throughout south-east Asia. You
can prepare your own from desiccated coconut or buy tins
of it from Indian stores.
  I have slightly adapted this recipe as certain ingredients
may be difficult to trace in your neighbourhood, but the
result is still delicious.

1kg (2lb) firm fish fillets, washed and dried and cut into 2.5cm (1in)
  squares

Marinade
450ml (¾ pint) coconut milk (see Santan page 251)
1 onion, thinly sliced
½ teaspoon chilli pepper
2 cloves garlic, crushed
½ teaspoon *terasi* dried shrimp paste (optional) (see p. 255)
1 teaspoon salt

2 strips lemon rind
½ teaspoon cumin
2 tablespoons chopped fresh basil OR 2 teaspoons dried basil
1 tablespoon chopped fresh mint OR 1 teaspoon dried mint

Garnish
lemon wedges

1 If preparing your own coconut milk, place the desiccated
coconut and water in a liquidizer and blend for 30 seconds.
Pour this mixture through muslin into a bowl. This should
produce about the required amount of milk.
2 Pour half of the coconut milk back into the liquidiser and
add the onion, chilli pepper, garlic, shrimp paste and salt.
Blend until the mixture is smooth. Pour into a shallow dish,
add the fish pieces, turn to coat and set aside for 30 minutes.
3 Thread the fish pieces on to skewers and grill over charcoal
for 5–8 minutes, turning occasionally. Do not overcook.
4 Meanwhile put the remaining marinade in a saucepan,
add the remaining coconut milk, the lemon rind, cumin,
basil and mint and simmer over a low heat, stirring
constantly.
5 Serve the kebabs on a bed of rice, spoon the sauce over the
top and serve with lemon wedges.

Sardines grillées au sauce cresson – sardine kebab with
watercress sauce

This is a popular recipe from southern France.
  Serve with potatoes, bread and a bowl of salad.
  A simple but very tasty dish.

1kg (2lb) fresh sardines, cleaned and washed in cold water
4 tablespoons olive oil
24 bay leaves

Sauce
2 bunches watercress, washed, shaken dry and finely chopped
2 tablespoons finely chopped parsley
300ml (½ pint) mayonnaise
½ teaspoon salt
½ teaspoon black pepper

1 Brush the sardines with the olive oil. Using flat skewers, thread the sardines on to six skewers alternating with bay leaves. Cook for 3–5 minutes, brush with a little more oil and then turn and cook for a further 5 minutes or until the fish are cooked and lightly browned.

2 Meanwhile mix the sauce ingredients together thoroughly in a bowl.

3 Serve the sardines immediately with the sauce.

In Turkey this recipe is usually prepared with anchovies, but sprats or sardines are equally suitable.

Caca kebabi – sprat kebab

This kebab also makes an excellent starter for a picnic.

I particularly like to dip the fish in tahina sauce or Turkish tarator sauce (see page 249).

1kg (2lb) sprats, cleaned and washed

Marinade
juice 2 large lemons
1 teaspoon salt
¼ teaspoon black pepper
1 teaspoon paprika
4 tablespoons oil
2 bay leaves
1 onion, cut into rings

Garnish
lemon wedges
olives, radishes and pickles

1 Place all the marinade ingredients together in a large bowl. Add the sprats and gently mix until they are well coated with the marinade. Cover and refrigerate for at least 2 hours.

2 Thread the sprats on to skewers – 3 to 4 per skewer depending on size. Grill over charcoal for 8–10 minutes, turning occasionally until the fish are crisp. Remove from the heat and transfer the fish to a large serving dish. Squeeze lemon juice over them and garnish.

Psari a Piraeus – Greek fish kebab with vegetables

From Piraeus, this traditional kebab is a rich mixture of fish and vegetables and makes a great use of oregano – a herb that goes extremely well with fish generally.

The ideal accompaniments are a fresh salad and a rice pilav of your choice and not forgetting a cold bottle of Retsina.

6 white fish steaks, cut into 3–3.5cm (1¼in–1½in) pieces
1 large green pepper, cut into 2.5cm (1in) squares
12 bay leaves
6 small firm tomatoes
6 button mushrooms, wiped clean

Marinade
75ml (2½fl oz) olive oil
150ml (¼ pint) dry red wine
juice 1 lemon
1 teaspoon salt
1 teaspoon dried oregano
1 clove garlic, finely chopped

Garnish
lemon wedges
bowl of dried oregano

1 Mix the marinade ingredients together in a large bowl. Add the fish pieces, turn until well coated and then cover and refrigerate for about 8 hours or overnight.
2 Thread the fish pieces on to skewers alternating with pieces of pepper, bay leaves, tomatoes and mushrooms. Grill over charcoal for about 10 minutes, turning and basting regularly with any remaining marinade.
3 Serve immediately on a bed of rice pilav accompanied by lemon wedges. Sprinkle a little oregano over the fish and use the bowl of oregano as a light dip.

Plaice kebab

A delightful combination of fish with bacon.
Particularly nice when served with potatoes and other vegetables.

15 rashers streaky bacon, rind removed
750g (1½lb) plaice fillets, skin removed

Marinade
150ml (¼ pint) dry white wine
2 tablespoons oil
½ teaspoon salt
½ teaspoon chilli pepper
¼ teaspoon white pepper
½ teaspoon sweet basil

Garnish
lemon wedges
spring onions and radishes

1 Using the back of a knife carefully stretch the bacon
rashers and then cut each one in half crossways.
2 Cut the fish into 30 pieces. Place each piece of plaice on a
halved bacon rasher, roll up and secure with a cocktail stick.
3 Mix all the marinade ingredients together in a shallow
dish. Arrange the bacon rolls in the dish, turning each one
until it is well coated. Cover and refrigerate for 1 hour.
4 Remove the rolls from the marinade and carefully thread
on to skewers – you can remove the cocktail sticks if you
like, but it is not necessary. Grill over charcoal for 8–10
minutes, turning and basting with the marinade
occasionally. Serve immediately with the garnish.

Saté udang – Sumatran prawn kebab

This prawn kebab, marinated in coconut milk and spices,
makes an excellent appetizer served on a bed of lettuce
leaves OR a main dish with a pilav of your choice.

1kg (2lb) prawns, shelled and de-veined

Marinade
4 tablespoons lemon juice
150ml (¼ pint) coconut milk (see Santan p. 251)
½ teaspoon chilli pepper
½ teaspoon dried shrimp paste (*terasi* – see page 255) crushed with
  the back of a spoon (optional)
1½ tablespoons soy sauce

1 teaspoon brown sugar
grated rind 1 lemon
1 clove garlic, crushed
1 teaspoon salt

1 Mix all the marinade ingredients in a large bowl. Add the
prawns, toss carefully in the marinade, cover and
refrigerate for about one hour.
2 Thread the prawns on to skewers and grill over charcoal
for about 5 minutes, turning frequently.
3 Meanwhile pour the remaining marinade into a small
saucepan and simmer over a low heat for 3–4 minutes,
stirring constantly.
4 Serve the kebabs either on a bed of lettuce leaves or on a
bed of rice pilav and pour the warmed sauce over them.

Scampi kebabs

These unusual kebabs made with prawns, or large shrimps,
peppers, bacon and mushrooms and flavoured with lemon,
garlic and sage, have a distinctly Mediterranean taste.
  Serve with saffron rice and a mixed green or tomato salad.

24 Dublin Bay prawns (or large shrimps), shelled
3 small green peppers, each cut into 8 pieces
8 rashers lean bacon, each cut into 3 pieces
24 button mushrooms, wiped clean
24 sage leaves, washed and shaken dry
3 lemons, quartered and with each quarter cut across in half

Marinade
60ml (2fl oz) olive oil
3 tablespoons lemon juice
3 cloves garlic, crushed
1 teaspoon salt
½ teaspoon black pepper

1 Mix the marinade ingredients together in a large bowl.
Add the prawns, stir well and set aside at room temperature
for about one hour, turning occasionally.
2 Remove the prawns from the marinade and thread all the

ingredients, evenly distributed, on to 6 skewers. Reserve the marinade.
3 Grill over charcoal for about 5–8 minutes, turning frequently.
4 Serve the kebabs with a little of the reserved marinade spooned over each.

Shellfish kebab

A rich mixture of ingredients, made the more interesting by the inclusion of mustard, ginger, horseradish and curry powder.
 Serve with a fried rice pilav.

750g (1½lb) shrimps, shelled and de-veined
12 oysters
6 lean bacon rashers
6 tomatoes, halved
1 large onion, cut into 2.5cm (1in) squares
1 large green pepper, cut into 12 pieces

Marinade
3 tablespoons soy sauce
2 tablespoons oil
1 small onion, finely chopped
1 tablespoon grated fresh ginger
1 clove garlic, crushed
1 teaspoon horseradish sauce
1 teaspoon dry mustard
½ teaspoon curry powder

1 Mix all the marinade ingredients together in a large bowl. Add the shrimps, turn gently to coat with the marinade and set aside at room temperature for 2–3 hours.
2 Puff the oysters slightly in hot water.
3 Grill the bacon gently for 2 minutes. Cut each rasher in half. Wrap the oysters in the half rashers of bacon and secure with toothpicks.

4 Remove the shrimps from the marinade. On each of six
skewers thread two oyster-bacon rolls and some shrimps
alternating them with two pieces green pepper, two tomato
halves and several slices onion. Grill over charcoal for 5–8
minutes, turning and basting frequently with the marinade.
While cooking, heat any remaining marinade to serve as a
sauce.
5 Serve each kebab on an individual plate on a bed of fried
rice pilav accompanied by the sauce.

Coquilles en brochette – scallop and bacon kebab

A highly prized French recipe, this is a dish of succulent
scallops alternated on skewers with bacon and peppers.

24 scallops
4 shallots, peeled and halved
2 sprigs parsley
1 teaspoon salt
½ teaspoon black pepper
300ml (½ pint) dry white wine
1 egg, lightly beaten
4 tablespoons fresh white breadcrumbs
8 rashers streaky bacon, rind removed
2 large green peppers, cut into 2.5cm (1in) squares
24 mushrooms wiped clean
oil

1 Slide the scallops from their flat shells and remove the
gills and black threads.
2 Place the scallops in a saucepan with the halved shallots,
parsley sprigs and salt and pepper. Add the wine and poach
the scallops over a gentle heat for about 7 minutes or until
tender. Lift out the scallops and cool.
3 Cut the orange roe out of each scallop and coat them in
the egg and breadcrumbs.
4 Cut each white scallop part in half horizontally.
5 Stretch each bacon rasher with the back of a knife and cut
each one into three. Wrap a piece of bacon around each
white scallop part.

5 Thread the scallops, both the coated roes and the bacon-wrapped white parts on to skewers alternating them with the pepper squares and mushrooms. Brush the kebabs with oil and cook for about 8–10 minutes, turning occasionally. Serve with a fresh salad and bread.

Pilavs

The rice plant is indigenous to Asia. Rice is the staple food of more than half the world's population and is the basic diet of such lands as China, India, Indonesia, Iran, Turkey, Madagascar and West Africa.

Most of the world's supply is grown in China and India. During the 17th century rice was introduced into the USA and cultivation started in Louisiana. Today the USA is the leading rice-exporting country.

Rice is therefore one of the staple ingredients of most of the 'kebab lands', and a bed of rice pilav is the perfect accompaniment to all kebabs. There are countless variations on the theme of rice. The recipes in this chapter are all for simple pilavs and come from a variety of kebab lands. Although rice is a simple grain the recipes chosen will, I am sure, prove that a touch of imagination, some experimentation and a true understanding of vegetables can make a big thing out of a grain of rice.

Also included are a few pilavs made with different grains, e.g. burghul (cracked wheat), cous-cous and kasha (buckwheat).

Roz – plain rice pilav

There are just about as many ways of cooking even plain pilav as there are cooks to cook it.

A general rule when cooking rice is to use:

2 cups of liquid for the first cup of rice and 1½ cups of liquid for every following cup of rice – volume is more important than weight.

The following is a fairly standard recipe used throughout the Middle East, though of course there are innumerable variations.

50g (2oz) butter
350g (12oz) long grain rice, washed thoroughly under cold running
  water and drained
1 teaspoon salt
900ml (1½ pints) boiling stock or water

1 Melt the butter in a medium saucepan over a moderate heat. Add the drained rice and fry, stirring constantly for 2–3 minutes. Add the salt and boiling stock or water and stir. Allow the mixture to boil vigorously for 2–3 minutes and then cover, lower the heat and simmer for 15–20 minutes or until all the liquid has been absorbed. The grains should be tender and separate and there should be small holes in the surface of the rice.
2 Turn off the heat. Remove the lid, cover the pan with a tea towel, then replace the lid. Set aside to 'rest' for 10–15 minutes.
3 Gently fluff up the rice with a long-pronged fork and serve.

Kasmag pilav – rice with pomegranates

This is something really different – a pilav from Azerbaijan in the Caucasus where the rice is cooked on a 'kazmag' – a thin round layer of dough. It is a colourful dish, being garnished with fresh pomegranate seeds.

1 egg
salt
75g (3oz) plain flour, sifted
2.5l (4 pints) stock or water
½ teaspoon ground saffron
350g (12oz) long grain rice, washed thoroughly under cold water
  and drained
½ tablespoon oil
100g (4oz) butter, melted
1 large ripe pomegranate

1 First prepare the kazmag. Beat the egg in a mixing bowl until frothy and add a pinch of salt. Add 50g (2oz) of the flour and mix well. Then add the remaining flour, a little at a time until the dough is smooth and does not stick to the fingers. Flour a working top and roll out the dough. Place a flameproof casserole on the dough and cut around it so that you have a piece of dough which will fit into the base of the casserole. Set the dough aside.

2 In a large saucepan bring the stock or water, saffron and 1 tablespoon of salt to the boil. Add the drained rice slowly so as not to disturb the boiling. Boil briskly for exactly 10 minutes, then drain into a colander.

3 Brush the base of the casserole with the oil and place the kazmag in the bottom. Brush liberally with some of the melted butter. Add the rice and sprinkle evenly with the remaining butter. Cover the casserole with a tea-towel (to absorb the steam) and the lid and cook over a very low heat for 35–45 minutes.

4 To serve pile the rice on to a large plate and garnish with wedges of the golden brown kazmag crust. Peel the pomegranate and sprinkle the seeds over the top.

African vegetable rice

An extremely colourful West African rice pilav. It is an ideal accompaniment for poultry or steaks.

350g (12oz) long grain rice, washed thoroughly under cold water
  and drained
900ml (1½ pints) water
2 teaspoons salt
50g (2oz) butter
1 onion, finely chopped
2 large tomatoes, blanched, peeled and chopped
1 large red pepper, chopped
2 sticks celery, trimmed and chopped
100g (4oz) mushrooms, chopped
100g (4oz) broccoli, chopped
1 teaspoon cayenne pepper

1 Put the rice in a large saucepan, add the water and 1½ teaspoons of the salt and bring to the boil. Cover the pan, lower the heat and simmer for 15 minutes or until the liquid is absorbed and the rice is tender. Remove the pan from the heat and set aside.

2 Melt the butter in a large frying pan, add the onion and fry for about 5 minutes or until the onion is soft but not brown. Add all the remaining vegetables and fry, stirring constantly, for about 2 minutes. Stir in the cayenne pepper and remaining salt.

3 Carefully add the rice and stir the mixture gently until the vegetables are evenly distributed. Cook for a further 8–10 minutes, stirring frequently. Serve immediately.

Sou tay taffan – Vegetarian fried rice

Here is a clever vegetarian dish from China which is also suitable for serving with any grilled meat.

6 eggs
1½ teaspoons salt
4 tablespoons oil
1 onion, finely chopped
stalks of 2 spring onions, cut into 1cm (½in) pieces
450g (1lb) cooked rice
75g (3oz) butter
1 medium aubergine, cut into ½cm (¼in) cubes
100g (4oz) peas
100g (4oz) mushrooms, roughly chopped
3 tablespoons soy sauce

1 In a small bowl beat the eggs lightly with the salt.

2 Heat the oil in a large pan, add the onion and spring onion stalks and fry for about 3 minutes until soft but not brown. Lower the heat, pour in the eggs, let them set and then slightly scramble them. Remove half the egg mixture and set aside.

3 Add the rice to the pan and mix it into the remaining egg and onion mixture. Cook gently, stirring frequently for 2–3

minutes until the rice is heated through and then remove from the heat.

4 Heat the butter in a frying pan, add the aubergine, peas and mushrooms and fry for 8–10 minutes or until the aubergines are soft, stirring frequently. Stir in the soy sauce and cook for a further 2–3 minutes. Tip this vegetable mixture into the rice and mix thoroughly.

5 Now place the pan of rice over a moderate heat, add the remaining egg and onion mixture and heat through, stirring gently.

Serve at once.

Pilav with pineapple and cashew nuts

This pilav is a subtle mixture of taste and texture and complements lamb and pork kebabs.

75g (3oz) butter
1 small pineapple, peeled, cored and cut into chunks
3 tablespoons raisins
12 spring onions, chopped
75g (3oz) cashew nuts
1 tablespoon coriander seeds, coarsely crushed OR 1 teaspoon ground coriander
¼ teaspoon chilli pepper
350g (12oz) long grain rice, washed thoroughly under cold water and drained
1 teaspoon salt
600ml (1 pint) chicken stock

1 Melt half the butter in a saucepan. Add the pineapple chunks and raisins and fry, turning frequently for 2–3 minutes or until the pineapple is lightly golden and the raisins are plump. Remove from the heat and set aside.

2 Melt the remaining butter in a large saucepan, add the spring onions and fry, stirring occasionally, for a few minutes until golden. Add the cashew nuts, coriander and chilli pepper and fry, stirring frequently for 2–3 minutes.

3 Add the rice and salt and fry for 5 minutes, stirring frequently. Stir in the pineapple-raisin mixture and the

stock. When the mixture is boiling vigorously cover the pan, reduce the heat and simmer for about 20 minutes or until the liquid has been absorbed and the rice is tender.
4 Leave to rest for 10 minutes, stir gently with a long-pronged fork and serve.

Chelo – Iranian rice pilav

The mainstay of the Iranian cuisine is rice in all its varieties and chelo rice is perhaps the jewel of them all.

Chelo can be served with many kinds of kebabs. It is usually heaped up on top of the meat. A pat of butter and a raw egg yolk are placed on top and sumac is sprinkled over all. Then it is all mixed up together and eaten with a spoon. The Persians also like to eat raw onion with their kebabs and to serve a thick slice of onion with each kebab.

350g (12oz) Basmati rice, washed very thoroughly under cold
  running water
2 tablespoons salt
50g (2oz) butter

To serve
6 pats of butter
6 raw egg yolks
1 large onion, cut into 6 rings
sumac (see page 255)

1 Place the drained rice in a large saucepan, add the salt and enough cold water to cover it by 2.5cm (1in). Leave to soak for 2 hours.
2 Bring 1.5l (2½ pints) water to the boil in a large heavy saucepan with a close fitting lid. Drain the rice thoroughly in a sieve and then pour it slowly into the water. Stir a few times and then boil, uncovered, for 5 minutes only. Drain the rice into a sieve.
3 Melt the butter in the large pan and add 150ml (¼ pint) water. Add the rice, cover the pan with a teatowel and then fit on the lid. Lift the ends of the towel onto the lid so that there is no danger of them catching fire. Cook the rice over a low heat for 15–20 minutes or until the grains are tender.

4 Stir up gently with a long-pronged fork and serve as described above.

Ararat pilav – rice with fruits

This must be one of the most spectacular rice pilavs of all. It makes a beautiful and dramatic centrepiece for a table, especially when it is lit in a darkened room.

Cooked rice – follow the recipe for Roz – plain rice pilav (p. 190)
50g (2oz) butter
75g (3oz) blanched almonds
100g (4oz) dried apricots, soaked overnight, drained and coarsely
  chopped
100g (4oz) stoned prunes, soaked overnight, drained and coarsely
  chopped
175g (6oz) raisins or sultanas
pinch ground cloves
25g (1oz) sugar
½ teaspoon cinnamon
2 apples
brandy

1 Prepare the rice according to the recipe for Roz. While it is resting, prepare the fruits.
2 Melt the butter in a saucepan, add the nuts, dried fruits, cloves and sugar and cook over a low heat, stirring frequently until the nuts are golden and the raisins or sultanas have puffed up. Sprinkle with the cinnamon and keep warm.
3 Core the apples and line the holes, including the bottom, with aluminium foil.
4 On a large serving platter pile the pilav into two separate peaks, a large one on the right and a smaller one on the left – this represents the shape of Mount Ararat.
5 Place the apples behind the peaks and fill the cores with brandy.
6 Arrange the fruit and nut mixture around the peaks to reach about halfway up the mountain leaving snow-capped peaks.
7 Lower the lights, ignite the brandy and serve.

Kesari chaval – saffron rice

This is the famous Indian saffron rice which is served in all self-respecting Indian restaurants.

100g (4oz) ghee or clarified butter
5cm (2in) cinnamon stick
6 cloves
2 large onions, thinly sliced
350g (12oz) Basmati rice, washed thoroughly under cold water and drained
900ml (1½ pints) boiling water
1 teaspoon salt
5 cardamom seeds
½ teaspoon saffron soaked in 2 tablespoons boiling water for 10 minutes

1 Melt the ghee or butter in a saucepan, add the cinnamon, cloves and onions and fry for 10 minutes, stirring frequently.
2 Add the rice and fry for a further 4–5 minutes or until every grain is a golden colour. Add the water, salt and cardamom seeds. When the mixture is boiling rapidly, reduce the heat to very low and stir in the saffron. Cover the pan and leave to simmer for about 20 minutes or until all the liquid has been absorbed. Leave to rest for a few minutes and then serve.

Rizi dhaktildhi – Greek rice mould

This is an attractive Greek pilav which is usually moulded into a ring and makes a superb accompaniment for Greek pork kebabs – Souvlakis.

1 teaspoon salt
2 teaspoons lemon juice
350g (12oz) rice, washed thoroughly under cold water and drained
3 tomatoes, finely chopped
3 tablespoons chopped chives
3 tablespoons chopped parsley
15 green olives, stoned and finely chopped
½ teaspoon basil

½ teaspoon marjoram
1 large red pepper, finely chopped
6 tablespoons olive oil
3 tablespoons vinegar
1 teaspoon salt
½ teaspoon black pepper

Garnish
Black olives

1 Bring about 1.5l (2½ pints) water to the boil in a saucepan
with the salt and lemon juice. Add the rice and cook for
12–15 minutes until the rice is just tender. Drain the rice
into a colander and cover with a clean cloth.
2 Put the tomatoes, chives, parsley, green olives, basil,
marjoram and red pepper into a large bowl and mix well.
Stir in the rice and mix until all the ingredients are well
distributed.
3 In a small bowl mix together the oil, vinegar, salt and
pepper and then stir into the rice mixture.
4 Press the rice into a ring mould and cover the mould with
buttered foil or greaseproof paper. Pour enough boiling
water into a roasting tin to reach a depth of 1cm (½in) and
place the mould in it. Cook over a gentle heat for 15
minutes.
5 Remove the mould from the tin and peel off the foil or
paper. Place a serving dish over the mould and invert.
Shake gently and the rice mould should slide out. Garnish
with the black olives and serve.

Coconut rice

This is a pilav from India. There is a Caribbean variation
which adds raisins and chopped nuts as well as coconut. The
raisins are sometimes soaked in rum first.

350g (12oz) rice, washed thoroughly under cold water and drained
3 tablespoons cooking oil
½ teaspoon black mustard seeds
2 tablespoons urd dhal (see p. 255)
75g (3 oz) desiccated coconut

1 Bring 1.2l (2 pints) of salted water to the boil in a large saucepan. Add the rice and simmer for 10–12 minutes or until the rice is about three quarters cooked – test by biting the grain, it should still have a hard centre. Drain into a colander.

2 In a heavy saucepan heat the oil, add the mustard seeds and fry, stirring frequently, until the seeds start to spit. Add the urd dhal and coconut and fry until brown, stirring constantly. Add the rice, reduce the heat, stir and add a little more salt if necessary. Cover and leave to steam for a further 10 minutes. Serve with fresh tarragon or curry leaves.

Roz-bil-tamar – rice and date pilav

This is a favourite dish in most Arab countries.

Ingredients as for Roz – plain rice pilav (p. 190)
50g (2oz) butter
75g (3oz) blanched almonds
100g (4oz) chopped dates
75g (3oz) raisins or sultanas
2 teaspoons rosewater

1 Cook the rice following the instructions for Roz. While the rice is resting, melt half the butter in a small pan. Add the almonds and fry, stirring frequently until they begin to turn golden. Add the remaining butter, the dates and raisins or sultanas and rosewater and fry gently for a further 3–4 minutes or until the almonds are golden and the fruit puffed up.

2 Spoon the rice on to a serving dish and sprinkle the fruit and nuts over the top.

Kari pollo – curried rice pilav

This Indian pilav is made with curry powder, onion and parsley. The Iranians add dried mint to it.

Although it can be served cold as a salad, I prefer my curry pilav hot and steaming.

Excellent with all kebabs.

50g (2oz) ghee or clarified butter
1 large onion, finely chopped
350g (12oz) long-grained rice, washed thoroughly under cold water and drained
2 teaspoons curry powder, or more to taste
3 tablespoons finely chopped parsley
1 teaspoon salt
1.5l (1½ pints) boiling stock or water

1 Melt the ghee or butter in a large saucepan, add the onion and fry until soft. Add the rice and fry for 2–3 minutes, stirring frequently. Add the curry powder, parsley and salt and mix well.
2 Add the boiling stock or water, boil vigorously for 2–3 minutes and then lower the heat and simmer for about 15–20 minutes or until all the liquid has been absorbed. Cover with a clean teatowel and set aside for 10–15 minutes. Fluff up with a long-pronged fork and serve.

Plain burghul pilav – cracked wheat pilav

Burghul is the Arabic name for cracked wheat. It is the basic cereal of Armenian cuisine and is served in any variety of ways.

It has been known for centuries and was produced in quantity in Mesopotamia. It is made by boiling whole grains of wheat until they soften. They are then dried – in the old days this would have been in the sun – and then crushed. It can be bought in Middle Eastern stores, health food shops and some large supermarkets. Make sure you buy the large or medium grain.

350g (12oz) large grain burghul
50g (2oz) ghee or butter
1 onion, finely chopped
600ml (1 pint) boiling stock or water
1 teaspoon salt

1 Put the burghul in a bowl or fine sieve and wash several times until the water runs clear, then leave to drain.

2 Melt the butter in a saucepan, add the onion and fry gently until soft and golden. Add the burghul and fry for 2–3 minutes, stirring constantly. Add the boiling water or stock and stir in the salt. Boil vigorously for 5 minutes, lower the heat and simmer, uncovered, for a further 8–10 minutes or until the liquid has been absorbed.

3 Turn off the heat, cover the pan with a tea-towel, fit on the lid and leave to rest for 10–15 minutes.

This is ideal to serve with any kebab as an alternative to rice. As with rice so with burghul there are many variations to the plain pilav and a very popular one is: *Burghul with Vermicelli*

Ingredients for Burghul Pilav above plus
50g (2oz) vermicelli, broken into 2.5cm (1in) pieces

Melt the butter in the saucepan, add the vermicelli and sauté until golden, stirring frequently. Add the burghul and proceed as with the above recipe.

Cous-cous – semolina pilav

Cous-cous is fine semolina which is made from wheat. It is the staple cereal of North Africa.

You can buy it from most continental stores and it is excellent with any kebab, particularly lamb and chicken.

450g (1lb) cous-cous
1 teaspoon ginger
1 teaspoon cumin
1 teaspoon coriander
1 teaspoon chilli pepper
50g (2oz) butter

1 Spread the cous-cous out on a baking tray and sprinkle generously with warm salted water. Work lightly between your fingers so that each grain is separated, moistened and beginning to swell. Set aside for 15 minutes.

2 Repeat this process twice more.

3 Half fill the bottom part of a couscousier with water. If you do not have one, a double saucepan or a saucepan over which a colander will fit snugly will do. Add all the spices and bring to the boil.

4 When the cous-cous is ready pour it into the top of the couscousier. If using a double saucepan or colander line with a fine teatowel first as the holes may be too large and the grains will fall through. Then add the cous-cous.

5 Place on top of the pan with boiling water, cover and simmer for about 30 minutes, fluffing up once or twice with a long-pronged fork.

6 Cut the butter into small pieces and stir into the cous-cous. Continue to steam for a further 15–20 minutes, fluffing up with the fork occasionally to ensure that all the grains are evenly coated.

Pile into a large dish and serve.

Kasha – buckwheat pilav

Kasha is an essential ingredient in many Russian recipes. The word, in its pure form, means cooked buckwheat, but today it is also applied to many other grains including rice, semolina, millet and oats.

For generations it was the staple food of millions. It is an extremely versatile food. It is eaten with milk for breakfast, with vegetables as a sustaining luncheon or is simply boiled and eaten with lots of butter. If you add a little chopped meat it becomes a family meal and with the addition of chicken livers, mushrooms and soured cream it becomes a sophisticated party dish.

To cook kasha

1 Preheat the oven to 180°C, 350°F, Gas Mark 4.

2 Lightly grease an ovenproof casserole with butter and set aside.

3 Put 225g (8oz) kasha or buckwheat into a saucepan (without any fat), set over a moderate heat and cook,

stirring constantly with a wooden spoon for 2 minutes.
4 Add 1 lightly beaten egg and stir until all the grains are
coated. Reduce the heat to low and cook for 2–3 minutes,
stirring constantly.
5 Transfer the mixture to the casserole and add:

1 tablespoon butter
½ teaspoon salt
450ml (¾ pint) boiling water

6 Stir well, cover the casserole and bake in the oven for
about 20 minutes.
7 Remove the dish from the oven. The kasha is now ready
to serve or to use in other recipes.
  A very good kasha pilav is the one below from the Ukraine
which makes an excellent accompaniment to lamb, beef or
veal.

Kasha with mushrooms and onions

50g (2oz) butter
1 large onion, finely chopped
350g (12oz) mushrooms, wiped clean and sliced
½ teaspoon salt
½ teaspoon black pepper
1 tablespoon finely chopped parsley
225g (8oz) kasha, cooked (see above)
4 tablespoons soured cream

1 Melt the butter in a large frying pan, add the onions and
fry, stirring frequently until soft but not brown. Add the
mushrooms and fry for another 3 minutes, stirring
occasionally.
2 Sprinkle the salt, pepper and parsley over the vegetables
and stir in the kasha. Lower the heat and cook for 10
minutes or until the kasha is thoroughly heated through.
3 Transfer the mixture to a serving dish and spoon the cream
over the top. Serve immediately.

Bread

'Man may live by bread alone
But kebabs without bread – never!' – Armenian saying

Bread has been, and still is the staff of life all over the world.
There are, perhaps as many kinds of bread as there are
cultures and civilisations, but there are only a few that go
well with kebabs. The breads chosen for this chapter
therefore come from those regions which are the kebab lands
i.e. the Middle East, Iran and the Indian sub-continent.
 The two outstanding breads that go with kebabs are *pita*
and *lavash*. Pita is the standard Middle Eastern bread now
popular all over Europe and sold in many shops. Its origin is
Syrian (*Khubs shami*) and it is ideal because, when it is cut
in half, its pocket can be filled with kebab and salad. In
Armenia and Iran where it is known as *Nan-e-Barbari* the
bread is sprinkled with sesame seeds before it is cooked.
 Lavash is a Caucasian bread and is, perhaps the most
perfect bread ever created. It is flat and round and can be
up to 60cm (2ft) in diameter, is about 3mm (⅛in) thick and
cooks in about 1 minute. It is also known as Lebanese
mountain bread, but it is generally found all over the Middle
East. It is normally cooked in a *Tonir* – basically an oven
in the ground or, as in times past in the floor of a house. A
pit is lined with bricks and the fire is laid directly on the
stones in the base. The Arabs have something similar where
they prepare the fire and cover it with a dome-shaped oven
made of cast iron.
 Two of the other breads chosen come from North India.
Chapatti and *paratha*, both now well known in the West,

are perfect for kebabs. The final bread is *non* which is from
Central Asia.

I have tried, where necessary, to simplify and modify the
ancient recipes to suit modern tastes and equipment.

Non – a flat onion bread

Non or *nan* is the word for bread in all the lands bordering
the Indian sub-continent. This particular bread is a speciality
from Central Asia. It is extremely popular in such little
known lands culinary-wise (or other-wise) as Uzbekistan,
Tadzhikistan and Kirkizia.

It has a wonderful taste and aroma and is ideal with any
kind of lamb kebab.

75g (3oz) butter
1 large onion, finely chopped
150ml (¼ pint) lukewarm water
1 teaspoon salt
350g (12oz) plain flour, sifted
vegetable oil

1 Melt 15g (½ oz) of the butter in a large frying pan. Add
the onion and fry for a few minutes until it is soft but not
brown. Transfer the onion to a large mixing bowl.
2 Melt the remaining butter in the pan and pour it into the
mixing bowl. Add the water and salt and mix well. Stir in
the flour a little at a time. Mix in with your hand. If the
dough sticks to your fingers then add a little more flour.
3 Lightly flour a work top, place the dough on it and knead
for several minutes until smooth and pliable. Gather into a
large ball and then divide it into 14–16 pieces. Roll each into
a ball.
4 On a floured working top roll out the balls with a rolling
pin, one at a time into circles about 17.5–20cm (7–8in) in
diameter.
5 Place a frying pan with a base at least 20cm (8in) in
diameter over a high heat. When it is hot enough (you can
test by flicking a few drops of water across its surface – they

should evaporate instantly) brush the surface with a little oil.
Reduce heat to moderate.
6 Place a circle of dough in the centre of the pan and cook
for about 4 minutes or until the underside is light brown.
Turn with a palette knife and cook the other side in the same
way. Remove and keep warm while you cook the remaining
circles of dough in the same way.
7 Serve immediately. If the nons are not all eaten at once
then store them in a dry place until needed and re-heat
under a hot grill for 2–3 minutes on each side.

Chapatti

The chapatti, made with wholemeal flour is the staple cereal
food of Northern India and, like most other Indian breads, is
unleavened.

225g (8oz) wholemeal flour
½ teaspoon salt
150ml (¼ pint) water
150ml (¼ pint) clarified melted butter

1 Sift the flour and salt into a large mixing bowl. Make a
well in the centre and pour in 90ml (3fl oz) of the water.
Draw the flour into the water with your fingers and mix well,
adding the rest of the water gradually. Form the dough into
a ball and place it on a floured working top.
2 Knead for about 10 minutes or until it has become smooth
and elastic. Put the dough into a clean bowl, cover with a
cloth and leave at room temperature for 30 minutes.
3 Divide the dough into eight portions and roll into balls.
On a floured surface roll out each ball of dough into a thin
round shape about 15cm (6in) in diameter.
4 Meanwhile heat a heavy iron frying pan or griddle and
when it is hot place one portion of the dough in the pan.
When small blisters appear on the surface press the chapatti
to flatten it. When the underside is pale golden turn it over
and cook the remaining side in the same way. Remove from

the pan and brush both sides with a little of the melted butter. Place on a plate and cover with another plate to keep it warm while you cook the other chapatti in the same way.

Serve warm.

Lavash

Lavash is the classic and probably the oldest form of bread found in the Caucasus. It is thin and crispy.

Below is a simplified version of lavash.

15g (½oz) fresh yeast or 8g (¼oz) dried yeast
lukewarm water
1 teaspoon sugar
450g (1lb) plain flour
1 teaspoon salt

1 Dissolve the yeast in 210ml (7fl oz) warm water. Stir in the sugar.

2 Sift the flour and salt into a large bowl. Make a well in the centre and slowly work in the dissolved yeast and enough warm water to make a stiff dough. Knead well on a floured work surface for about 10 minutes until smooth and elastic. Place the ball of dough in a clean bowl, cover with a cloth and leave in a warm place for at least 3 hours.

3 Transfer the dough to a floured surface, punch it down and knead again for a few minutes. Return to the bowl, cover and leave for a further 30 minutes.

4 Flour the working surface again and then divide the dough into apple-sized lumps. With a long rolling pin roll out each ball into a thin sheet about 20–25cm (8in–10in) in diameter. Sprinkle the surface with more flour occasionally to prevent sticking.

5 Line the bottom of the oven with aluminium foil. Heat the oven to 200°C, 400°F, Gas Mark 6.

6 Place each sheet of dough on the foil in turn and cook for about 3 minutes. Cover the cooked *lavash* with a cloth to keep warm while the remaining ones are being cooked. Serve immediately.

Paratha

This is the standard bread found in any Indian restaurant.
It is a speciality of North India and is a must with any
tandoori-based kebab and excellent with any Middle Eastern
kebab.

450g (1lb) wholewheat flour
1 teaspoon salt
300ml (½ pint) water
225g (8oz) butter or ghee – ghee is preferable as it has a distinctive
   flavour

1 Sift the flour into a large mixing bowl. Make a well in the
centre and pour in half the water. Mix with your fingers
and gradually add the rest of the water until the dough is
firm. Form into a ball and transfer to a floured work surface.
Knead for about 10 minutes or until the dough becomes
smooth and elastic. Place in a clean bowl, cover with a cloth
and set aside at room temperature for about 30 minutes.
2 Divide the dough into eight portions and roll each one into
a ball between your palms. Taking one at a time, roll in
flour and then roll it out as thinly as possible on a floured
surface.
3 Melt the ghee or butter and brush it over the upper surface
of the dough. Fold the dough and re-form it into a ball again.
Roll it out into a circle about 15cm (6in) in diameter and 1cm
(½in) thick.
4 Heat a large heavy frying pan and pour in a little of the
melted butter. Add a paratha and fry on both sides until
golden and crisp. Keep hot while you cook the remaining
parathas in the same way, adding more butter as required.
Serve hot.

Pita

This is the ideal bread for eating with kebabs. You can make
it or buy it from delicatessens and many supermarkets.
   It is a flat bread which is hollow and thus makes a perfect

edible food container and does away with the need for plates.
When your kebab is ready to be eaten, warm the pita, insert
a sharp knife and slit it half open. Place a little salad in
the opening and then slip in the kebab and eat as you would
a sandwich.

The Armenian version of this bread includes the addition
of sesame seeds. When the dough is shaped, coat the surface
of the loaves with a little beaten egg and sprinkle generously
with sesame seeds. Bake as with the plain pita.

15g (½oz) fresh yeast OR 8g (¼oz) dried yeast
about 300ml (½ pint) tepid water
pinch sugar
450g (1lb) plain flour
½ teaspoon salt
oil

1 In a small bowl dissolve the yeast in 3–4 tablespoons of
warm water. Stir in the sugar and leave in a warm place
for 10–15 minutes or until it becomes frothy.
2 Sift the flour and salt into a large mixing bowl. Make a
well in the centre and pour in the yeast mixture. Add
enough tepid water to make a firm but not stiff dough. Gather
the dough up and transfer to a lightly floured work surface.
Knead for about 10 minutes or until smooth and elastic. If
you knead in 1 tablespoon of oil it will make a softer bread.
3 Wash and dry the mixing bowl and lightly oil it. Roll the
dough round and round the bowl until it is greased all over
– this will prevent the dough from going crusty and cracking
while rising. Cover the bowl with a damp cloth and leave
in a warm place for 2–3 hours or until it has doubled in size.
4 Punch the dough down and knead for a further minute or
two. Divide the dough into 8 portions and roll each between
your palms until round and smooth.
5 Lightly flour a board and flatten each one out on it with
the palm of your hand or with a rolling pin until it is about
½cm (¼in) thick and as even and circular as possible. Place
the rounds close to each other, but not touching. Dust them
with flour and cover with a floured cloth. Leave to rise for
20–30 minutes.

6 Preheat the oven to 230°C–240°C, 450°F–475°F, Gas Mark
8–9, putting in two large oiled baking sheets halfway
through the heating period. When the oven is ready, slide
the rounds of dough on to the hot sheets, dampening the
tops to prevent them browning. Bake for 10 minutes and do
not open the oven door during this time. After 10 minutes
it is safe to open it cautiously to see if the pitas have puffed
up. Put on to wire racks to cool as soon as you remove them
from the oven. They should be soft and white with a pouch
inside.

Salads

With most of the salads there is an emphasis on simple
vegetables such as potatoes, beans, cucumbers, mushrooms,
tomatoes etc., but I quickly came to realise that there was
no escape from the aubergines and courgettes which are
ideal with kebabs and some of these are included in the
chapter on Cooked Vegetables. In order to achieve a
successful blend with the hot, marinated, charcoal-cooked
meats it is necessary to have simple salads without too
many spices. Olive oil, olives, tahina, lemon juice, cumin,
salt, pepper, mint and parsley are some of the ideal dressing
ingredients for a successful salad that will taste perfect on
its own and yet complement the main dishes, be they lamb,
beef, fowl or fish barbecues.

I have been rather biased towards the Mediterranean region
simply because that is where salads are at their best. I have
been rather surprised to find that the people of the Far East
do not go much for cold salads. They prefer to serve lightly
cooked vegetables. This also applies to the Indian sub-
continent where hot cooked vegetables are more popular.
As for the exotic salads of the Caribbean Islands, they use
many fruits and vegetables that are not so ready available
in Europe although they are slowly being introduced.

Now a few words on the laying out of salads. Arrange the
dishes in such a way that the colours, harmonies and
contrasts of the vegetables are at their best and most
appetising. So instead of preparing large quantities of one
salad it is better to make smaller portions of a few, thus
enriching the table without incurring wastage. It is also
very usual at Middle Eastern kebab meals to serve small

dishes of black and green olives, cubed white cheese, small gherkins, radishes, pickles and fresh herbs such as parsley, chives, mint, dill, spring onions and coriander.

Jajig – yoghurt and cucumber salad

This famed yoghurt-cucumber salad is a must with kebabs.
600ml (1 pint) yoghurt
½ teaspoon salt
1 clove garlic, crushed
1 cucumber, peeled and finely chopped
2 tablespoons finely chopped fresh mint OR 1 teaspoon dried mint

Garnish
A pinch of chilli pepper

1 Place the yoghurt in a mixing bowl and stir in the remaining ingredients. Refrigerate until ready to use.
2 To serve pour into small individual bowls and sprinkle with a little chilli pepper.

A variation is *Raeta* which is the general name given to a yoghurt-based fruit or vegetable dish in India.

The standard *raeta* found on the menus of most Indian restaurants in the West is very much like the Middle-Eastern *jajig*, but the following recipe goes further than the yoghurt-cucumber concept and makes clever use of mangoes. Bananas, aubergines and potatoes can be used in the same way.

600ml (1 pint) yoghurt
2 ripe, fresh mangoes, peeled, stoned and diced. You can use drained, tinned ones instead.
½ teaspoon salt
1 tablespoon ghee
1 tablespoon mustard seeds
1 green chilli, finely chopped

Garnish
2 teaspoons finely chopped coriander leaves

1 In a mixing bowl beat the yoghurt until smooth. Add the mangoes and salt and set aside.

2 Melt the ghee in a small pan and when it is hot add the mustard seeds and fry until the seeds begin to pop. Add the chilli and fry, stirring constantly for 10 seconds. Tip the contents of the pan into the yoghurt mixture and stir well. Cover and refrigerate.

3 Before serving sprinkle with the coriander leaves.

Aqurki ou rukescia grietne – soured cream and cucumber salad

This salad is from the Baltic.

Soured cream, smetana, is a common ingredient in Eastern European cooking and here it is used interestingly with mustard.

You can substitute yoghurt if you wish.

1 large cucumber, peeled
2 teaspoons salt
1 teaspoon vinegar
3 hard-boiled eggs
1 teaspoon French mustard
150ml (¼ pint) soured cream
2 teaspoons wine vinegar
¼ teaspoon sugar

To serve
lettuce leaves
1 tablespoon fresh dill OR 1 teaspoon dried dillweed

1 Cut the cucumber in half lengthways and then cut into ½cm (¼in) pieces. Put into a mixing bowl and sprinkle with the salt and teaspoon of vinegar. Stir well and set aside for 30 minutes.

2 Drain the cucumber and pat dry with kitchen paper. Place in a large bowl.

3 Separate the yolks and whites of the hard-boiled eggs. Cut the whites into thin slices and stir into the cucumber.

4 Mash the egg yolks and rub them through a fine sieve into a small bowl. Add the mustard, soured cream, vinegar and

sugar and stir until the mixture is smooth. Pour over the cucumber and mix well.

5 To serve arrange the lettuce leaves around a large plate and heap the salad into the centre. Sprinkle with the dill.

Cucumber and olive salad

Another Middle Eastern salad making use of two local ingredients. Dazzlingly simple, it is perfect with steaks or lamb kebabs.

1 cucumber, peeled and thinly sliced
50g (2oz) black olives, stoned and sliced.

Dressing
2 tablespoons lemon juice
1 tablespoon olive oil
½ teaspoon salt
2 tablespoons dried mint

Garnish
50g (2oz) feta cheese, crumbled. You can buy this cheese from many
  delicatessens and some large supermarkets. However you can
  substitute Lancashire or white Stilton

1 Place the cucumber and olive slices in a bowl.
2 Mix the dressing ingredients together and pour over the vegetables. Mix together and spoon into a salad bowl. Sprinkle with the cheese and serve.

Apple and celery salad

This is a Caucasian salad using honey as a contrast to the piquancy of the celery.
  Ideal with pork and chicken kebabs.

4 sticks of celery
4 large eating apples
2 tablespoons honey
3 tablespoons lemon juice
4 tablespoons chopped walnuts
2 tablespoons finely chopped parsley

1 Wash and trim the sticks of celery and cut into small pieces.
2 Peel, core and slice the apples. Place in a bowl with the celery.

Mix the honey and lemon juice together in a small bowl and pour over the celery and apple slices. Stir well and spoon into a salad bowl. Sprinkle with the walnuts and parsley and serve.

Potato and corn salad

A popular American salad

1kg (2lb) potatoes (new ones are especially tasty), boiled and cooled
small tin, approx 225g (8oz), sweetcorn, drained
1 bunch spring onions

Dressing
4 tablespoons mayonnaise
1 teaspoon Worcestershire sauce
1 heaped tablespoon cucumber relish

1 Cut the cold potatoes into chunky pieces and put into a large bowl. Add the sweetcorn.
2 Trim the roots and outer leaves from the onions and cut into slices. Add to the other vegetables.
3 Mix the dressing ingredients together in a small bowl and pour over the vegetables. Toss lightly and chill before serving.

Avocado and walnut salad

A clever use of avocado, which has only recently been introduced into the Middle Eastern cuisine, and walnuts which are an indigenous crop. This mixture of old and new is very refreshing and delightful in appearance. This is an Israeli recipe.

2 large avocados, stoned and peeled
3 tablespoons lemon juice
1 onion, finely chopped
4 pickled cucumbers, thinly sliced

2 sticks celery, chopped
100g (4oz) shelled walnuts, quartered
1½ teaspoons salt
½ teaspoon black pepper
1 large red pepper, thinly sliced
50g (2oz) black olives, stoned
1 teaspoon cumin

1 Cube the avocado flesh, place in a bowl and sprinkle with the lemon juice. Add the onion, cucumber, celery and walnuts. Season with the salt and pepper, toss and refrigerate for 30 minutes.
2 Before serving garnish the salad with the pepper strips and olives and sprinkle with the cumin.

Orange and olive salad

This is another interesting salad from Israel making use of her prized commodity – oranges. Personally, I do not think that kirsch is as suitable as *filfar* which is an orange liqueur from Cyprus available in most wine shops. However, why not try both and make up your own mind.

An excellent salad with veal and, dare I say it, pork!

3 oranges, peeled and segmented
75g (3oz) black olives, stoned and sliced
75g (3oz) green olives, stoned and sliced
½ teaspoon salt
¼ teaspoon chilli pepper
2 tablespoons olive oil
½ teaspoon cumin
3 tablespoons kirsch or filfar

1 Cut each orange segment into about three pieces. Put into a bowl and add all the remaining ingredients. Mix thoroughly, cover and refrigerate.
2 Spoon into a serving dish and serve.

Salad hollandaise – spinach, apple and cheese salad

With an interesting combination of ingredients this salad goes well with grilled steaks.

3 large eating apples
juice 1 lemon
225g (8oz) Edam cheese, rind discarded and cheese diced
1 small tin pimentos, drained and cut into thin strips
450g (1lb) fresh spinach, washed very thoroughly under cold
  running water

Dressing
3 tablespoons vinegar
4 tablespoons olive oil
½ teaspoon dry mustard
½ teaspoon sugar
1 teaspoon salt
½ teaspoon black pepper

1 Peel and core the apples, then dice them. Place in a bowl,
add the lemon juice and toss well. Stir in the prepared
cheese and pimentos.
2 Discard the stems of the spinach and any coarse leaves.
Tear the remaining leaves into 5cm (2in) pieces.
3 Mix all the dressing ingredients together in a large bowl.
Add the spinach and mix well. Remove the spinach with a
slotted spoon and arrange it around the edge of a shallow
salad dish.
4 Add the apples, cheese and pimentos to the remaining
dressing and toss well. Pile this mixture into the centre of
the dish and serve.

Salad-e-saltanati – kidney bean and potato salad

This 'Royal Salad' makes an interesting use of red kidney
beans – a favourite in Iran – with mayonnaise and eggs.

175g (6oz) red kidney beans, soaked overnight in cold water OR one
  350g (12oz) tin
450g (1lb) potatoes, cooked in their skins, cooled and peeled
6 tablespoons olive oil
3 tablespoons lemon juice
6 tablespoons mayonnaise
1 lettuce, finely shredded
1 large onion, thinly sliced

salt and pepper to taste
2 hard-boiled eggs, shelled

Garnish
1 tablespoon sumac (see p. 255)

1 Drain the soaked beans and place in a large saucepan. Add
enough boiling water to cover by 5cm (2in) and simmer
until the beans are tender, adding more boiling water if
necessary. Drain and cool. If using tinned beans then simply
drain.
2 Dice the potatoes into a salad bowl.
3 In a small bowl mix together the oil, lemon juice and
mayonnaise. Pour this dressing over the potatoes. Add the
beans, lettuce and onion and mix well. Season to taste with
the salt and pepper. Finely chop the eggs and sprinkle them
and the sumac over the salad. Serve immediately or the
lettuce will become limp.

Mdzhavai kombosto – red cabbage salad

This red cabbage salad from the Caucasus – reputedly a
favourite of Stalin – is made with a white cabbage pickled
in a marinade for a week until it turns red.

1 small white cabbage, trimmed of any coarse outer leaves
1kg (2lb) beetroot, peeled and cut into 2.5cm (1in) pieces
10 sprigs parsley, stalks cut off
1 head celery, leaves only
600ml (1 pint) red wine vinegar
2 teaspoons paprika

1 Put the cabbage into a large casserole or saucepan, cover
with cold water and bring to the boil. Lower the heat and
simmer for 45 minutes.
2 Remove the cabbage and place it in a colander to drain
and to cool.
3 When cool enough to handle gently pull back first the outer
leaves and then the inner ones thus giving the cabbage the
appearance of a large rose. Place in a large casserole.

4 Add the remaining ingredients to the casserole and pour in enough water to cover the cabbage by about 5cm (2in). Place a heavy plate on top of the cabbage to hold it under the liquid and set aside for 1 week.
5 Remove the cabbage from the liquid, drain and set upright on a plate. Cut into wedges and serve.

Insalata di funghi – mushroom salad

This salad is from Italy.

450g (1lb) button mushrooms, wiped clean and thinly sliced
100g (4oz) cooked peas

Dressing
6 tablespoons olive oil
2 tablespoons lemon juice
½ teaspoon salt
¼ teaspoon black pepper

To serve
1 crisp lettuce, shredded

1 Place the sliced mushrooms and peas in a bowl.
2 Mix the dressing ingredients together thoroughly in a small bowl and pour over the vegetables. Toss well and refrigerate for 30 minutes.
3 Line a serving dish with the shredded lettuce. Pile the mushroom and pea mixture into the centre and serve immediately.

Mixed green salad

The best salad with any barbecue. You can add other vegetables of your choice and you can sprinkle over chopped hard-boiled eggs, grated cheese, a few black olives, sultanas or chopped nuts.

2 heads Cos lettuce, washed thoroughly and shaken dry
175g (6oz) peas, cooked until just tender
1 small cucumber, thinly sliced

1 stick celery, thinly sliced
4 spring onions, trimmed and thinly sliced

Dressing
4 tablespoons oil
4 tablespoons white wine vinegar
2 tablespoons finely chopped parsley
1 clove garlic, crushed
1 teaspoon salt
½ teaspoon black pepper
½ teaspoon oregano
½ teaspoon paprika

1 Shred the lettuce finely and place in a salad bowl with the remaining vegetables.
2 In a small bowl mix all the dressing ingredients together thoroughly.
3 When ready to serve the salad pour the dressing over the vegetables and toss well. Serve immediately.

Ensalada de zanahorias – Mexican carrot salad

You can adjust the amount of hot chillies according to your taste.

450g (1lb) carrots, peeled and grated
1 small tin pineapple chunks
2 tablespoons raisins
50g (2oz) sunflower seeds
juice 1 small lemon
2 teaspoons wine vinegar
150ml (¼ pint) soured cream or yoghurt
½ teaspoon salt
½ teaspoon dill seeds
½ teaspoon chilli pepper
2–3 chillies, seeded and thinly sliced

To serve
Shredded lettuce

1 Place all the ingredients in a large bowl and mix thoroughly.

2 Arrange the lettuce leaves on a serving dish and pile the salad on top of them. Serve immediately.

Patates salatasi – potato and tomato salad

This salad is a favourite in Turkey and Armenia.

6 large potatoes, cooked and cut into 1cm (½in) cubes
4 tomatoes, quartered and with each quarter cut in half

Dressing
2 cloves garlic, crushed
3 tablespoons oil
juice 1 large lemon
1 teaspoon salt
½ teaspoon black pepper
2 tablespoons finely chopped parsley

1 Mix the prepared potatoes and tomatoes in a large bowl.
2 In a small bowl mix all the dressing ingredients together. Pour over the vegetables and toss well. Taste and adjust the seasoning if necessary.
3 Chill for 30 minutes before serving.

Domates salatasi – tomato salad

This salad is undoubtedly the most popular one in Turkey and probably throughout the Middle East.

6 tomatoes, thinly sliced
100g (4oz) mixed black and green olives
2 large green peppers, thinly sliced
3 tablespoons finely chopped parsley
4 tablespoons lemon juice
3 tablespoons olive oil
Salt and pepper to taste.

1 On a large oval serving dish arrange the tomato slices down the centre. Arrange the olives down one side and the pepper slices down the other. Sprinkle with the parsley.
2 Make a dressing of the lemon juice, oil, salt and pepper. Pour evenly over the vegetables and serve.

Coleslaw

This famous salad is excellent with all grills and is
particularly good with hamburgers, sausages etc.

There are many variations on the basic recipe below. You
can add raisins, chopped dates, roasted peanuts, cress and
sliced fruits.

450g (1lb) white cabbage, finely shredded
3 medium carrots, peeled and grated
1 red pepper, thinly sliced
1 onion, thinly sliced
6 tablespoons mayonnaise
1 teaspoon salt
¼ teaspoon black pepper

Place all the vegetables in a large bowl and stir in the
mayonnaise. Season with the salt and pepper and then taste
and adjust seasoning if necessary. Chill for 1 hour, then
serve.

Cooked vegetables

What can one do with vegetables? Boil them, fry them, bake them, steam them or stew them in oil. In the main 'kebab lands', i.e. the Middle East and the Indian sub-continent, people tend to fry or stew vegetables rather than boil them. Why? Perhaps because they have discovered over the centuries that vegetables cooked in this way retain their flavour and goodness and perhaps too because the people of the Middle East and those living on the shores of the Mediterranean sea have that wonderful oil made from olives – one of the most versatile of all ingredients. Most of the dishes cooked in oil taste as delicious cold as they do hot. The Indians too have their beloved ghee, which is clarified butter. I have chosen certain vegetables that I believe go well with barbecues. These are aubergines, courgettes, beans, mushrooms, okra, carrots, cauliflower and potatoes. Needless to say any vegetables can be suitable or be made to suit a barbecue, but I believe that in the list above there will be sufficient to accompany and enhance the flavour of a kebab and yet still stand on their own merits.

Aubergines, courgettes and okra are native to the kebab lands and I think that the cuisines of the Middle East and India really know how to exploit the qualities of these three vegetables. All that you need to produce an interesting dish are the vegetables, spices, herbs, oils, nuts and sometimes fruit. Quite simple! In fact that is the secret of good and successful cooking. As the sage once put it – 'Simplicity is the deepest and grandest of all aims – and almost impossible to achieve.'

Ch'ao lou sun – stir-fried asparagus

This is one of the countless Chinese stir-fried vegetable recipes. You can cook any other vegetable of your choice in the same way. Some particularly suitable ones are broccoli, aubergines, bamboo shoots, cabbage, carrots, peppers and mushrooms.

750g (1½lb) asparagus, tough stem ends removed
3 tablespoons peanut or any other nut oil
1½ teaspoons salt
1 level teaspoon sugar
2 tablespoons water

1 Scrape each asparagus stalk and then cut into 2.5cm (1in) pieces. Drop the pieces into a bowl of lukewarm water and leave for 15 minutes. Pour off the water, rinse and drain.
2 If you have a wok so much the better, otherwise use a shallow saucepan or a frying pan. Heat the oil in it, add the asparagus and stir-fry over a high heat for 2–3 minutes. Add the salt, sugar and water, stir well and fry for 2 more minutes.
3 Remove the asparagus from the pan and serve.

Aubergine basquaise

A tasty combination of aubergines, tomatoes, onion and peppers which goes particularly well with lamb kebabs.

2 large aubergines, wiped clean
2 teaspoons salt
120ml (4fl oz) oil
1 large onion, thinly sliced crossways and pushed out into rings
1 green pepper, thinly sliced
1 red pepper, thinly sliced
6 large tomatoes, blanched, peeled and chopped
100g (4oz) mushrooms, wiped clean and sliced
1 teaspoon dried basil
1 teaspoon black pepper

Garnish
1 tablespoon finely chopped parsley

1 Cut the aubergines into thin slices, place them in a
colander and sprinkle with the salt. Set aside for 30 minutes
and then pat dry with kitchen paper.
2 Heat half the oil in a large frying pan, add some of the
aubergine slices and fry until golden, turning once. Remove
and keep warm while you fry the remaining slices in the
same way. Add more oil if necessary.
3 When all the slices are cooked and removed, heat any
remaining oil in the pan and add the onion and peppers.
Fry for about 5 minutes or until soft. Add the remaining
ingredients and cook gently for 5–10 minutes.
4 Carefully stir in the aubergine slices. Reduce the heat to
low, cover the pan and simmer, stirring occasionally for 15
minutes.
5 Turn the vegetables into a serving dish, sprinkle with the
parsley and serve.

Creole green beans

Excellent with all barbecues.

1kg (2lb) green beans or mange-tout peas, topped and tailed
2 teaspoons salt
50g (2oz) butter
1 small onion, finely chopped
1 small green pepper, finely chopped
5 level tablespoons tomato ketchup
juice 1 lemon
1 green chilli, finely chopped
1 level tablespoon curry powder
1 level tablespoon French or English mustard

1 Half fill a large saucepan with water and bring to the boil.
Add the beans and salt and simmer for 5–10 minutes or
until the beans are tender but still firm. Drain and set side.
2 Melt the butter in a large pan and fry the onion and pepper,
stirrig regularly until soft. Add all the remaining
ingredients except the beans and cook for 5 minutes, stirring

frequently. Mix in the beans, lower the heat and simmer for a further 5 minutes.

Serve immediately.

Frijoles negros – Cuban black beans

Beans are very popular throughout Latin America and the Caribbean. This simple recipe is ideal with all grills.

450 (1lb) black beans (red kidney beans will do as well), soaked overnight
6 tablespoons oil
1 onion, finely chopped
2 cloves garlic, chopped
1 large green pepper, chopped
2 bay leaves
1½ teaspoons salt
½ teaspoon black pepper
½ teaspoon chilli pepper
½ teaspoon cumin

1 Drain the beans and place in a large saucepan. Add enough water to cover by about 5cm (2in) and bring to the boil. Simmer for 1–2 hours or until the beans are tender, adding more boiling water if necessary. Drain.
2 Heat the oil in a large pan, add the onion, garlic and green pepper and fry for several minutes, stirring frequently until soft.
3 Add the beans and remaining ingredients and mix well. Cover the pan and cook for a further 10–15 minutes.

Serve hot or cold.

Gazar mughrabi – carrots with cumin and thyme

This is a spicy and unusual way to serve carrots which comes from Algeria. It is equally delicious hot or cold.

1kg (2lb) carrots, scraped and cut crossways into 1cm (½in) slices
5 tablespoons oil

1 teaspoon salt
½ teaspoon white pepper
½ teaspoon cinnamon
½ teaspoon cumin seeds
3 cloves garlic, finely chopped
½ teaspoon dried thyme
1 bay leaf
1 tablespoon lemon juice

1 Place the carrots in a saucepan. Add enough water to cover
by about 2.5cm (1in) and bring to the boil. Simmer for about
15 minutes or until tender but still firm. Using a slotted
spoon remove the carrot slices and transfer them to a bowl.
Retain 150ml (¼ pint) of the cooking liquid.
2 In a medium saucepan mix together the oil, salt, pepper,
cinnamon, cumin seeds, garlic and thyme. Cook over a low
heat for 10 minutes. Add the reserved cooking liquid and the
bay leaf, cover the pan and simmer for 15–20 minutes.
3 Add the carrots, toss them in the sauce and cook for a
further 2–3 minutes or until the carrots are heated through.
Sprinkle in the lemon juice, remove the bay leaf and serve
immediately if to be eaten hot.

Shesh-andaz-e-havij – carrots with fruits

This Iranian dish makes something more of the humble
carrot with the help of dried fruits and pomegranate juice.
Try it as a change from boiled carrots. Particularly good with
pork and poultry kebabs.

750g (1½lb) carrots, peeled and cut into thin sticks
50g (2oz) butter
2 onions, finely chopped
50g (2oz) raisins or sultanas
100g (4oz) dates, stoned and chopped
3 tablespoons pomegranate syrup (page 255); if not available use
    vinegar
1½ teaspoons salt
25g (1oz) slivered almonds

1 Melt the butter in a large pan, add the carrots and fry for 2–3 minutes. Add the onions and fry until they are golden, stirring frequently.
2 Stir in the dried fruits, pomegranate syrup or vinegar and the salt. Cover and cook over a low heat for about 20–30 minutes or until the carrots are tender. Spoon the mixture into a serving dish and sprinkle the almonds over.

Lubia-el-fez – white beans with egg and saffron

A dish from Morocco which not only looks exotic, but smells of the souk or kasbah – and it tastes nice too!

450g (1lb) white beans, cannellini, flageolet or haricot, soaked overnight in cold water. Canned ones will also do, but if you use them buy 2 tins – each approx 350g (12oz)
1 onion, finely chopped
1 clove garlic, finely chopped
600ml (1 pint) water
150ml (¼ pint) oil
25g (1oz) chopped parsley
1½ teaspoons salt
¼ teaspoon saffron diluted in 1 tablespoon warm water
½ teaspoon black pepper
3 eggs

Garnish
2 tablespoons finely chopped parsley

1 Drain the soaked beans and place in a saucepan with the onion, garlic and water. Bring to the boil, cover and simmer until the beans are tender. Add a little more boiling water if necessary. If using canned beans use only 180ml (6fl oz) water and simmer for only 20–30 minutes.
2 In a small pan heat the oil and then stir in the parsley, salt, saffron mixture and pepper. Add this to the bean mixture, stir well and simmer for a further 10–15 minutes or until the remaining water has evaporated.
3 Break the eggs into the mixture, stir and when the eggs are just cooked serve immediately garnished with the parsley.

Engouyzov lupia – green beans in walnut sauce

This recipe is from the Caucasus. It is excellent with pork and poultry dishes.

450b (1lb) French beans, trimmed and cut into 5cm (2in) pieces
75g (3oz) shelled walnuts
2 cloves garlic, chopped
1 small onion, finely chopped
3 tablespoons chopped fresh coriander
½ teaspoon ground coriander
2 tablespoons olive oil
2 tablespoons wine vinegar
1 tablespoon lemon juice
a little chicken stock
2 tablespoons paprika
1½ teaspoons salt
1 tablespoon finely chopped parsley

Garnish
Pinch chilli pepper

1 Bring a large saucepan half filled with lightly salted water to the boil. Add the beans and cook briskly for 8–10 minutes or until the beans are just tender. Drain and leave to cool.
2 In a blender or mortar crush the walnuts and garlic to a paste. Scrape the paste into a large bowl and add the onion, coriander, oil, vinegar, lemon juice, paprika and salt and mix well. The mixture needs to have a very thick creamy consistency and so if you think it is too dry then add a little chicken stock. Taste and adjust the seasoning if necessary.
3 Add the beans and mix gently until well coated with the sauce. Lightly stir in the parsley and pile into a serving bowl. Sprinkle with the chilli pepper and serve.

Sambal goreng kembang kubal – spicy cauliflower

This fascinating cauliflower dish is from Indonesia where the intricate use of spices and the contrasting taste of sweet and sour have been far better exploited than in Europe and America.
  The spice *laos* (root of the Greater Galingale) is available

in powdered form in some continental stores, but if you cannot find it do not let that stop you proceeding with the recipe.

6–8 tablespoons peanut oil
2 onions, finely chopped
3 cloves garlic, finely chopped
6 red chillies, finely chopped
1 teaspoon *laos* – if available (p. 254)
½ teaspoon *terasi* – if available (p. 255)
1 tablespoon brown sugar
1 teaspoon salt
3 bay leaves
1 large cauliflower OR 2 small ones, broken into small florets
1 tablespoon lemon juice
450ml (¾ pint) thick *santan* (see page 251)

1 Heat the oil in a large saucepan and fry the onions, garlic, chillies, *laos*, *terasi*, brown sugar, salt and bay leaves for about 5 minutes or until the onion is soft.
2 Add the cauliflower and lemon juice, stir well and cook gently for 5–7 minutes.
3 Add the santan and simmer until the cauliflower is tender and the sauce thick.

Domatesli karnabar – Cauliflower in tomato sauce

A Balkan favourite which is excellent with lamb and beef grills.

3 tablespoons oil
1 large onion, finely chopped
1 clove garlic, finely chopped
750g (1½lb) tomatoes, blanched, peeled and chopped
450ml (¾ pint) water
2 teaspoons salt
1 teaspoon marjoram or basil
½ teaspoon dillweed
½ teaspoon black pepper
1 large cauliflower, broken into florets

Garnish
2 tablespoons finely chopped parsley or tarragon

1 Heat the oil in a small pan, add the onion and garlic and fry for a few minutes until soft. Transfer to a blender, add the tomatoes and water and purée.
2 Transfer the purée to a large saucepan and add the salt, marjoram or basil, dillweed and black pepper and bring to the boil. Drop in the cauliflower florets, cover the pan and simmer for 8–10 minutes or until the florets are just tender.
3 Transfer to a serving dish and sprinkle with the parsley or tarragon. Serve warm.

Courgettes en casserole

The courgettes in this dish are flavoured with herbs. They go well with any fish or meat dish.

50g (2oz) butter, melted
6 medium courgettes, washed, topped and tailed
1 onion, thinly sliced
1 tablespoon dried mint
½ tablespoon tarragon
½ tablespoon chives
1½ teaspoons salt
½ teaspoon black pepper

1 Brush a large shallow ovenproof dish with a little of the melted butter.
2 Cut the courgettes crossways into 1cm (½in) thick slices. Arrange the courgettes and onion slices in the dish. Pour the remaining melted butter evenly over the vegetables. Sprinkle the remaining ingredients over the top.
3 Cover the dish and bake in an oven preheated to 180°C, 350°F, Gas Mark 4, for about 30 minutes or until the courgettes are tender but not overcooked.

Yerevani gaghamp – Yerevan-style cabbage

Use red cabbage if it is available, but white cabbage will do. This dish goes well with all meat kebabs.

Quinces are seasonal fruit which are at their best around October-November. If not available use large cooking apples instead.

1kg (2lb) red or white cabbage
3 tablespoons butter
2 large quinces or cooking apples, cored and sliced
3 spring onions, finely chopped, including their bulbs
2 cloves garlic, finely chopped
 juice 1 lemon
1 teaspoon honey
1 teaspoon orange blossom water
2 teaspoons salt
½ teaspoon black pepper
½ teaspoon dillweed
½ teaspoon nutmeg

1 Remove any coarse and damaged outer leaves of the cabbage and cut out the core. Shred the leaves finely.
2 Melt the butter in a large saucepan, add the cabbage and fry for 5 minutes, turning occasionally to coat with the butter.
3 Add all the remaining ingredients and mix thoroughly. Cover the pan, lower the heat and cook for 20 minutes.
 Serve warm.

Bhindi sat tamatar – Okra with tomatoes

Okra (also known as 'ladies' fingers') is a finger-shaped, slightly hairy, sticky fruit pod. It is best exploited in the Middle Eastern, Indian and North African cuisines.

This simple recipe from the Indian sub-continent is typical of the many vegetable dishes that usually accompany a kobob or dry curry.

Buy small fresh okra. Large ones are often stringy.

750g (1½lb) small fresh okra, washed
50g (2oz) butter or ghee
1 large onion, finely chopped
6 large tomatoes, blanched, peeled and chopped
2 cloves garlic, finely chopped
2 cloves
2–3 bay leaves
1 level tablespoon ground coriander
1½ level tablespoons garam masala
1½ teaspoons salt
juice ½ lemon

1 Trim down the stems of the okra, but take care not to cut
into the flesh or the juice will escape.
2 Melt the butter or ghee in a large saucepan, add the onion
and fry for several minutes until soft. Add the tomatoes,
garlic, cloves, bay leaves, coriander, garam masala and salt
and stir well. Add the okra and toss gently to coat with the
sauce. Bring to the boil, cover the pan, lower and heat and
cook for 10–15 minutes or until the okra are just tender.
Do not overcook or the okra will become too soggy and
shapeless.
3 Sprinkle in the lemon juice and then turn into a serving
dish.

Batatas Portuguese – Portuguese potatoes

You can of course serve jacket or roast potatoes, but I suggest
you try this tasty and filling dish. It is particularly good
with grilled fish.

1kg (2lb) large potatoes, peeled
3 tablespoons oil
1 large onion, finely chopped
1 clove garlic, crushed
750g (1½lb) tomatoes, blanched, peeled and chopped
1½ teaspoons salt

1 Half fill a large saucepan with lightly salted water and
bring to the boil. Add the potatoes, simmer for 10 minutes

and then drain. When cool enough to handle slice them
thickly and set aside.
2 Heat the oil in a large frying pan, add the onion and garlic
and fry for several minutes until soft. Add the tomatoes and
salt and simmer for 3–4 minutes.
3 Add the potato slices, turn to coat with the sauce and bring
to the boil. Lower the heat, cover the pan and cook for about
a further 10 minutes or until the potatoes are tender. Do not
overcook or the slices will break up. Serve warm or cold.

Ch'ing chiao hsien ku – fried peppers and mushrooms

Although delicious made with button mushrooms, Chinese
cooks would prefer to use 'winter mushrooms' (*Tung Ku*) or
'black mushrooms' (*Hsien Chun*).

4 tablespoons peanut or corn oil
3 large green peppers, cut into 2.5cm (1in) squares
750g (1½lb) button mushrooms, wiped clean and stems discarded
½ teaspoon salt
2 teaspoons sugar
3 tablespoons soy sauce
60ml (2fl oz) water

1 Heat a wok or large saucepan. Add the oil and peppers and
fry for 5 minutes, stirring regularly.
2 Add the mushrooms and fry for a further 2–3 minutes. Stir
in the remaining ingredients, cover the wok or pan and cook
for 5 minutes.
 Serve immediately.

Baked pawpaw

Pawpaw (or papaya) is treated as a vegetable when unripe
and as a fruit when ripe. It is much loved and used in South
American and Caribbean cooking.
 This is a fine dish which goes well with pork and poultry
grills.

3 average green pawpaws
50g (2oz) butter
1 large onion, finely chopped
4 tomatoes, blanched, peeled and chopped
1 teaspoon salt
½ teaspoon black pepper
½ teaspoon garam masala
¼ teaspoon chilli pepper
100g (4oz) fresh breadcrumbs
75g (3oz) grated cheese

1 Half fill a saucepan with lightly salted water and bring to the boil.
2 Halve the pawpaws lengthways and scoop out and discard the seeds. Drop the pawpaws into the water and simmer for 15 minutes. Drain.
3 When cool enough to handle, scoop out the flesh and reserve it and the shells.
4 Heat half the butter in a frying pan, add the onion and fry for several minutes until soft. Stir in the tomatoes, chopped reserved pawpaw flesh, salt, pepper, garam masala and chilli pepper. Fill the reserved shells with this mixture.
5 Arrange these shells side by side in a large shallow ovenproof dish. Mix the breadcrumbs and cheese together and sprinkle evenly over the pawpaw halves. Dot with the remaining butter.
6 Bake in an oven preheated to 180°C, 350°F, Gas Mark 4, for about 20 minutes or until the topping is golden.
 Serve immediately.

Calabaza curry – pumpkin curry

This West Indian dish with Indian overtones is usually prepared with a local pumpkin called *calabaza*, but any pumpkin or vegetable marrow will do.

3 tablespoons oil
100g (¼lb) lean bacon, chopped
1 onion, finely chopped
1 green pepper, chopped
1 teaspoon curry powder

½ teaspoon chilli pepper
1 teaspoon garam masala
3 large tomatoes, blanched, peeled and chopped
2 cloves garlic, crushed
1½ teaspoons salt
750g (1½lb) pumpkin or marrow, peeled. Cut flesh into 2.5cm (1in)
  cubes

1 Heat the oil in a large saucepan, add the bacon, onion and
pepper and fry for several minutes until soft. Stir in the
curry powder, chilli pepper and garam masala and cook for
1 minute.
2 Add all the remaining ingredients and stir thoroughly.
Cover the pan and simmer for about 20 minutes or until
the pumpkin is tender.

Hung shao pai lo po – Chinese braised turnips

A clever and tasty way of preparing the humble turnip.
 Goes well with all barbecue dishes.

1kg (2lb) turnips, peeled and cut into 2.5cm (1in) cubes
3 tablespoons peanut or corn oil
2 teaspoons sugar
3 tablespoons soy sauce
6 tablespoons water

1 Half fill a large saucepan with lightly salted water and
bring to the boil. Add the turnip cubes and cook for 5
minutes. Drain and reserve.
2 Heat a wok or large saucepan and add the oil. When hot
add the turnip cubes and fry for 2 minutes, stirring
regularly. Add the sugar and soy sauce and cook for a further
2 minutes, stirring constantly.
3 Add the water and bring to the boil. Cover the pan, lower
the heat and simmer for about 30 minutes or until the
turnips are tender. Stir occasionally and serve hot.

Ghalieh esfanaj – spinach in pomegranate juice

Spinach with the piquancy of pomegranates is unbeatable with lamb.

175g (6oz) whole lentils, rinsed
25g (1oz) butter
1 onion, thinly sliced
750g (1½lb) spinach, coarse leaves and tough stems discarded, washed thoroughly
1 teaspoon salt
3 tablespoons pomegranate juice (p. 255)

1 Half-fill a large saucepan with lightly salted water and bring to the boil. Add the lentils, lower the heat and simmer for 30–40 minutes or until tender. Drain and set aside.
2 Melt the butter in a large saucepan, add the onion and fry, stirring frequently, until golden. Shake excess water from the spinach and chop coarsely. Add to the pan, stir well, cover and cook for 10 minutes.
3 Stir in the lentils, salt and pomegranate juice, cover the pan and cook for a further 15–20 minutes. Transfer to a large dish and serve immediately.

Plantains in coconut milk

This recipe is from the West Indies.
  Plantains are green bananas which are used only in cooking. You can find them in most Indian grocery stores.
  This fascinating dish goes extremely well with grilled pork, chicken and fish.

6–8 plantains
50g (2oz) butter or margarine
1½ teaspoons garam masala
1½ teaspoons salt
½ teaspoon black pepper
1 small onion, finely chopped
600ml (1 pint) thick coconut milk (santan p. 251)
2 eggs, beaten

Garnish
1 teaspoon paprika

1 Peel the plantains and slice lengthways. If they are long
cut each slice in half.
2 Melt the fat in a large frying pan, add the garam masala,
salt, pepper and onion and fry for several minutes, stirring
frequently until soft. Add the plantain slices and fry, turning
carefully, for 2 minutes until golden.
3 Gradually pour in the coconut milk and stir carefully.
Lower the heat and simmer for 20–30 minutes. Remove pan
from the heat and stir in the beaten eggs. Serve when the
eggs have set.
4 Turn into a serving dish, sprinkle the paprika over the top
and serve.

Marinades, sauces and dips

Cooking meat and fish on a barbecue adds a new dimension to the flavour of the flesh since the aroma of the smoke penetrates and enhances it. But this is not enough. By basting and marinating and with the additional use of sauces and dips other aspects are created.

Basting is the brushing of flavoured oil or fat over the meat while it is cooking. This deepens the flavour and helps prevent the flesh drying, but it does not permeate the flesh.

Marinating is the keeping of meat or fish for several hours or longer in a flavoured mixture. The acids from eg wine, vinegar and lemon help to tenderise the meat while the vegetable oil, olive oil or butter adds moisture. The seasonings eg salt, pepper, garlic and other spices and herbs add extra flavour.

Most kebabs have their own marinades and so the sauces and marinades included in this chapter for the most part are additional to the ones given in the previous chapters. Some are old, tried and tested (eg apple sauce and mint sauce) but you might like to try them with dishes other than those with which they are traditionally associated.

Trinidad barbecue marinade

This rich fascinating sauce has everything going for it – as well as in it! It is ideal with steaks.

90ml (3fl oz) oil
2 tablespoons wine vinegar
240ml (8fl oz) water
1 tablespoon Worcestershire sauce
1 small onion, finely chopped
1 chilli pepper, seeded and finely chopped
1 clove garlic, crushed
1 tablespoon brown sugar
½ tablespoon mustard powder
1 teaspoon salt
½ teaspoon black pepper
½ teaspoon thyme
½ teaspoon sage
1 teaspoon chopped parsley
1 teaspoon chopped chives
½ teaspoon oregano
½ teaspoon marjoram
½ teaspoon tabasco sauce

1 Put all the ingredients in a large bowl and mix well. Add the meat, turn to coat thoroughly and set aside at room temperature for 2–4 hours.
2 While the meat is cooking heat the remaining marinade in a small pan and simmer for 10 minutes
 Serve the meat with the sauce.

Everyman's barbecue marinade

This popular marinade goes well with meat, fish and poultry. It is simple and effective.

75ml (2½fl oz) oil
75ml (2½fl oz) dry sherry
2 tablespoons soy sauce
1 teaspoon Worcestershire sauce
1 clove garlic, crushed
½ teaspoon salt
¼ teaspoon black pepper

1 In a large bowl mix all the marinade ingredients together. Add the meat, fish or poultry, turn to coat, cover and refrigerate for 8–10 hours or overnight.

2 Use any remaining marinade as a baste while the meat or fish is cooking.

Tomato-soy marinade

A garlic-based tomato sauce that goes well with lamb kebabs.

150ml (¼ pint) tomato juice
juice 2 lemons
3 tablespoons soy sauce
1 teaspoon salt
1 clove garlic, crushed
½ teaspoon cumin

1 Combine all the ingredients in a large bowl. Add the lamb, turn and leave to to marinate for 6–8 hours.
2 Use any left-over marinade to baste the meat while cooking.

Herb marinade

This lovely marinade is Mediterranean in origin and is suitable for both lamb and beef kebabs.

180ml (6fl oz) olive oil
90ml (3fl oz) white wine
1 onion, finely chopped
2 cloves garlic, crushed
1 teaspoon each of thyme, basil and oregano
1 tablespoon fresh chives, chopped
8 black peppercorns, crushed
2 bay leaves
1 teaspoon salt

1 Mix all the ingredients together in a large bowl. Add the meat and turn to coat thoroughly. Cover and refrigerate for several hours or overnight.
2 Use any remaining marinade to baste the meat while it is cooking.

Pineapple and mustard sauce

This sauce, inspired by the Far East, can also be used as a marinade and baste for poultry, pork, lamb or fish.

300ml (½ pint) dry white wine
2 tablespoons white wine vinegar
2 tablespoons oil
300ml (½ pint) crushed pineapple – fresh or tinned
1 tablespoon soy sauce
1 tablespoon finely chopped onion
2 tablespoons brown sugar (use only 1 if using tinned pineapple)
1 teaspoon dry mustard
1 clove garlic, crushed
1 teaspoon lemon juice

1 Combine all the ingredients in a saucepan and mix well. Bring to the boil, lower the heat and simmer for 15 minutes.
2 Pour into a sauceboat and serve with the kebabs of your choice.
3 If you use it as a marinade leave the meat in it for 6–8 hours before cooking.

Mint sauce

This famed sauce needs no introduction. I have included it firstly because I like it and secondly because I do think we should experiment. In other words, why use it just with roast lamb? Try it with Shish Kebab or Barbecued Lamp Chops.

1 small handful of mint leaves
2 teaspoons caster sugar
3 tablespoons boiling water
3 tablespoons vinegar

1 Wash and dry the mint leaves and then chop them finely. Place in a small bowl and sprinkle with the sugar. Add the boiling water and vinegar, stir and leave to cool for 30 minutes.
  Serve as a side relish.

Rum sauce

For all kinds of poultry, game and pork.

1 tablespoon butter
1 tablespoon flour
300ml (½ pint) water
3 tablespoons sugar
150ml (¼ pint) white wine
juice ½ lemon
1 glass rum

1 Melt the butter in a small saucepan. Add the flour and stir until smooth. Gradually add the water, stirring constantly to avoid lumps. Sprinkle in the sugar. Simmer for a few minutes, stirring constantly until the sauce thickens.
2 Remove from the heat and stir in the wine, lemon juice and rum.
3 Re-heat and serve immediately.

Sauce bercy

A classic sauce, ideal with lamb, beef and fish.
  Below is a slightly simplified version.

75g (3oz) unsalted butter, melted
1 small onion, finely chopped
300ml (½ pint) dry white wine
2 teaspoons plain flour
2 tablespoons double cream
1 tablespoon finely chopped parsley
salt and pepper to taste

1 Pour half the melted butter into a small saucepan, add the onion and fry gently until soft. Add the wine and simmer until the liquid is reduced by half.
2 In a small bowl mix together the rest of the melted butter and the flour. Add a little of the pan liquid, stirring constantly to thin the mixture. Pour this into the saucepan and stir constantly until the sauce thickens.
3 Stir in the cream, parsley and salt and pepper to taste, but do not let the sauce boil or it will curdle.
  Serve immediately.

Sauce tartare

There is no need to explain or justify the inclusion of this famed sauce. It is simply a MUST with any fish kebab.

300ml (½ pint) mayonnaise
1 small onion, grated or very finely chopped
1 tablespoon vinegar
25g (1oz) green olives, chopped
1 tablespoon chopped capers
3 cocktail gherkins, finely chopped
1 teaspoon chopped chives
1 tablespoon double cream

1 Combine all the ingredients together in a bowl.
2 Serve as an accompaniment to grilled fish.

Cho kan jang – sesame sauce

Serve this sauce from Korea with cooked or raw vegetables as well as with grilled beef or pork.
  It is made with 'prepared sesame seeds' which are mentioned in several recipes.

175g (6oz) sesame seeds
2 tablespoons sugar
6 tablespoons vinegar
8 tablespoons light soy sauce

1 Remove any sand from among the seeds and then wash in a fine sieve. Place them in a frying pan and brown slowly, stirring constantly for about 5 minutes.
2 Crush with a mortar and pestle or in a grinder.
3 Place in a small bowl and mix in the sugar, vinegar and soy sauce.
4 Serve either as a dip in individual bowls or pour over the grilled meats.

Horseradish butter

This tangy butter makes an excellent accompaniment for grilled fish.

100g (4oz) butter, softened
4 tablespoons grated fresh horseradish
¼ teaspoon cayenne pepper

1 Mix the ingredients together in a bowl with a wooden
spoon until well blended. Chill for 30 minutes before
serving. You can divide and mould the mixture into
individual pats if you wish.

Creole sauce

I like this sauce for its rich flavour. It is excellent with lamb
and beef.

2 tablespoons oil
1 small onion, finely chopped
1 green pepper, thinly sliced
1 clove garlic, crushed
450g (1lb) tomatoes, blanched, peeled and chopped
2–3 chilli peppers, seeded and chopped
1 tablespoon sugar
1 teaspoon salt
½ teaspoon black pepper

1 Heat the oil in a saucepan, add the onion, green pepper
and garlic and fry for 5–8 minutes or until the onion is soft
but not brown.
2 Add the remaining ingredients and simmer for about 15
minutes. Serve immediately.

Vishniovy sous – cherry sauce

This Russian recipe is a good accompaniment for venison,
turkey, goose or any game bird.

225g (½lb) ripe cherries
2 tablespoons sugar
300ml (½ pint) chicken stock
¼ teaspoon cinnamon
4 cloves
1 teaspoon cornflour
1 glass dry sherry

1 Stone the cherries. Place them in a saucepan and mash.
Add the sugar, stock, cinnamon and bruised cloves. Bring
to the boil, lower the heat and simmer for about 10 minutes.
2 Mix the cornflour with 1–2 tablespoons of water to form a
smooth paste and add to the sauce. Bring to the boil, stirring
constantly and them remove from the heat.
3 Rub the sauce through a sieve, stir in the sherry and pour
over the carved meat.

Sukhdorov madzoon – garlic-yoghurt sauce

A garlic-yoghurt sauce from Armenia which goes extremely
well with fried vegetables e.g. aubergines and courgettes as
well as with lamb and beef kebabs.

300ml (½ pint) yoghurt
1 clove garlic, crushed
½ teaspoon salt
½ teaspoon crushed dried mint OR 2 tablespoons finely chopped
  fresh mint
¼ teaspoon chilli pepper

1 Mix the yoghurt, garlic, salt and mint together in a bowl.
Pour into a serving dish and sprinkle with the pepper.

Hunter's orange sauce

This sauce from the Bahamas makes use of oranges and
guava jelly. I have replaced the guava – for obvious reasons
– and recommend redcurrant jelly or, better still, honey.
  Use with all kinds of poultry or game kebabs.

25g (1oz) bacon fat (or any other fat)
25g (1oz) plain flour
240ml (8fl oz) water
1 teaspoon salt
½ teaspoon black pepper
½ teaspoon cayenne pepper
240ml (8fl oz) orange juice
grated rind of 4 oranges

1 tablespoon honey or redcurrant jelly or guava jelly if available
15g (½oz) butter
1 tablespoon rum

1 Melt the fat in a small saucepan, stir in the flour and then
gradually add the water, stirring constantly until you have
a smooth paste.
2 Add the salt, pepper, cayenne pepper, orange juice and
three-quarters of the orange rind, stirring all the time.
3 Next add the honey or jelly, butter and rum. Simmer for
5 minutes. Serve in a sauceboat with the remaining orange
rind sprinkled over the top.

Mutabal – aubergine and tahina dip

This aubergine and tahina appetiser is a must with any lamb
or poultry kebab. It is one of the classics of the Middle
Eastern kitchen. It is served as a dip. Most usually pita or
lavash bread is served with it, but be daring enough to dip
your pieces of kebab in it – I do and it is delicious!

2 large aubergines
3 cloves garlic, crushed
1 teaspoon salt
60–90ml (2–3fl oz) tahina paste
juice 2 lemons
1 teaspoon chilli pepper
1 teaspoon cumin
1 tablespoon olive oil
2 tablespoons finely chopped parsley
a few black olives for the garnish

1 Make two or three slits in each aubergine with a sharp
knife and cook them over charcoal, under the grill or in a
hot oven until the skins are black and the flesh feels soft
when poked with a finger. Allow to cool.
2 Peel off the skin, scraping off and keeping any flesh which
comes off with the skin. Put all the flesh into a large bowl and
mash with a fork. Add the crushed garlic and salt and
continue to mash or pound until the mixture is reduced to
a pulp.

3 Add the tahina, lemon juice and chilli pepper and stir thoroughly. Spoon the mixture onto a large plate, smooth it over and sprinkle with the cumin. Dribble the oil over the top and garnish with the parsley and olives.

Teradot – walnut and tahina dip

This is a Cilician (Southern Turkey) speciality which makes use of the two outstanding products of the region, namely tahina paste and walnuts.
 This goes well with fish kebabs.

175g (6oz) shelled walnuts
2 cloves garlic
6 tablespoons tahina paste
juice 2 large lemons
1 teaspoon cumin
4 tablespoons chopped parsley
1 teaspoon salt

Garnish
1 teaspoon paprika

1 In a blender or with a mortar and pestle grind the walnuts and garlic with just enough water to form a thick paste. Scrape into a mixing bowl.
2 Add all the remaining ingredients and mix thoroughly until well blended. Serve on a large plate garnished with the paprika.

Vinegar-soy dip

This is a popular sauce in the Far East, especially in Korea and Japan. It is often served as a dip.

6 tablespons soy sauce
6 tablespoons vinegar – malt or wine
2 tablespoons sugar
1 tablespoon pine nuts, chopped

1 Mix the soy sauce, vinegar and sugar together. Pour into one dish or into very small individual ones and sprinkle the chopped nuts over the top.
2 Either use as a dip or pour over the cooked meat.

Tarator – walnut dip

This sauce is ideal with grilled mussels, fish or chicken. It is Caucasian-Turkish by origin and is a must on any Turkish dining table. It is usually served as a dip in small individual bowls.

Armenians use pine kernels instead of walnuts. You can try a combination of the nuts to make an interesting alternative.

100g (4oz) walnuts or pine kernels
4 cloves garlic
1 teaspoon salt
4 slices white bread, crusts removed
2 tablespoons olive oil
juice 2 lemons

1 If using walnuts blanch them first and remove the skins. Grind the nuts, garlic and salt in a blender or pound with a mortar and pestle.
2 Meanwhile soak the bread in a little water, squeeze out and crumble into a bowl. Add the ground nut mixture together with the oil and lemon juice. Mix together to form a smooth thick sauce.
3 Serve in small individual bowls as an accompaniment to the main course.

Kuah saté 1

This spiced peanut sauce from Indonesia is a must with all satés. There is, however, no reason why you cannot serve it with other kebabs.

Serve in individual small bowls or pour over the saté or kebab.

4 red chillies, very finely chopped
450g (1lb) shelled fried peanuts, crushed
salt to taste
75ml (2½fl oz) peanut oil – if unobtainable use vegetable or olive
 oil
1 tablespoon brown sugar
¼ teaspoon *kentjur* – (page 254) if not available use Chinese five
 spice powder from any Chinese store or omit completely
1 tablespoon lemon juice

1 Mix all the ingredients together in a large bowl. Gradually
add sufficient boiling water, stirring constantly, to form a
sauce which is smooth and thick but thin enough to pour.

Kuah saté 2

This is a more elaborate sauce based on kuah saté 1 and
therefore the uses and preparation are similar.

450g (1lb) raw peanuts, shelled
75ml (2½fl oz) peanut oil or vegetable or olive oil
1 small onion, finely chopped
1 clove garlic, crushed
salt to taste
450ml (¾ pint) *santan* – see opposite
1 tablespoon brown sugar
½ teaspoon *kentjur* (see p. 254)
½ teaspoon *terasi* (p. 255)
1 tablespoon lemon juice
4 red chillies, very finely chopped
2 tablespoons *ketjap* (p. 254)

1 Blanch the raw peanuts by pouring boiling water over
them and then removing the skins. Crush the peanuts in a
blender or mortar and pestle.
2 Heat the oil, add the onion, garlic, salt, *santan*, sugar,
kentjur, terasi and lemon juice and fry gently for 5 minutes,
stirring frequently.
3 Stir in the peanuts, chillies and *ketjap* and fry for a further
10 minutes. Serve as with kuah saté 1.

Santan

This is one of the most important ingredients in the Indonesian cuisine. It is basically a coconut sauce made from grated fresh coconut which is then mixed with hot milk.

225g (½lb) grated fresh coconut *or* desiccated coconut
600ml (1 pint) milk

1 Put the coconut and milk in a saucepan and bring to the boil. Simmer for 15–20 minutes. Remove from the heat and allow to cool.
2 Pour into a fine sieve and squeeze out as much liquid as possible. Use as recommended in satés and Kuah Saté 2.

Tahiniyeh – tahina and cumin dip

This Middle Eastern sauce is usually used with fried or grilled fish, but there is no reason why it cannot accompany lamb, beef or even vegetables e.g. aubergines.

150ml (¼ pint) tahina paste
juice 2 large lemons
2 tablespoons olive oil
150–300ml (¼–½ pint) water or milk or a mixture of the two
2 cloves garlic, crushed
1 teaspoon salt
½ teaspoon black pepper
1 teaspoon cumin
2 tablespoons finely chopped parsley

1 Pour the tahina into a bowl. Add the lemon juice and stir. The mixture will become very stiff. Stir in the olive oil.
2 Slowly add the water or milk, a little at a time, stirring constantly until the sauce has a thick creamy texture.
3 Season with the garlic, salt, pepper, cumin and half the parsley. Stir in well, taste and adjust the seasoning if necessary.
4 Pour into a serving bowl or very small individual dishes and garnish with the remaining parsley.

Japanese dipping sauce

A very popular sauce with fish, chicken and beef. Has a sweetish flavour with a bite!

150ml (¼ pint) Japanese soy sauce
75ml (2½fl oz) *mirin* (p. 255) or dry sherry
3 teaspoons sugar
1 teaspoon grated fresh ginger

1 Mix the ingredients in a small saucepan and heat gently until the sugar has dissolved. Leave to cool.
2 Divide among very small individual bowls.

Podina chutney – mint chutney

This fascinating chutney from India keeps for a few days when refrigerated. However it is at its best when freshly prepared.

If fresh mint is not available use dried. You can also substitute 3 medium fresh green chillies well chopped for the chilli pepper. Dried pomegranate seeds are easily available in Indian groceries. Ask for 'Anardana'.

8 spring onions, washed and with outer leaves discarded
1 sprig fresh mint OR 1 tablespoon dried mint
1 level teaspoon chilli powder
1 teaspoon salt
1 teaspoon sugar
½ teaspoon garam masala
1 tablespoon dried pomegranate seeds – or enough fresh seeds to fill
  2 tablespoons
2 tablespoons lemon juice

If using fresh mint wash it under cold running water and shake dry. Coarsely chop the spring onions. Pass through a mincer together with the mint. Transfer to a mortar, add the chilli powder, salt, sugar and garam masala and pound for several minutes to reduce to a paste. Spoon into a small bowl. Crush the pomegranate seeds in the mortar and then stir thoroughly into the mint mixture. Add the lemon juice and mix well.

Serve with kebabs of your choice.

Apple sauce

This beautiful English-inspired sauce is made with cooking apples, a little sugar and a pinch of cinnamon

450g (1lb) cooking apples, peeled and cored
1 tablespoon sugar
½ teaspoon cinnamon

Place the whole apples in a saucepan with a little water and the sugar. Bring to the boil, lower the heat, cover the pan and simmer until soft. Turn the apples occasionally. Drain and set aside to cool a little.

Slice thinly or chop finely, place in a small bowl and sprinkle with the cinnamon.

Glossary

Arak Indonesian wine made from fermented rice

Burghul Cracked wheat.

Garam masala A spice mixture containing black pepper, cardamom, cinnamon, cloves, nutmeg, black cumin, coriander, bay leaf. Can be purchased ready-mixed from many shops.

Ghee Clarified butter. Can be obtained from some Indian grocers, or you can make it at home by heating unsalted butter gently until it melts. Strain through muslin, and keep until needed in the refrigerator.

Harissa A hot North African sauce which can be bought in small tins from most Continental, Indian and Middle Eastern stores

Kemiri nuts Also known as candlenuts, these are almost impossible to find in Europe. They have a hard shell and are similar in appearance to Brazil nuts. You can use Brazil nuts or walnuts instead.

Kentjur A powdered spice related to ginger and turmeric. Can be bought from shops specialising in Indonesian ingredients, or you can substitute Chinese five-spice powder.

Ketjap manis An Indonesian speciality virtually unknown outside the archipelago. It is sweetened soya bean sauce. As a substitute, use 1 teaspoon of honey mixed with 4 tablespoons soya bean sauce. Make sure the soya bean sauce is the thick variety which is sold in all Chinese stores.

Laos The dried and powdered root of the greater galangal plant, with a gingery taste, frequently used in Indonesian cooking. Can be bought in shops specialising in Far Eastern foods.

Mango juice can be bought in tins, or occasionally fresh, from Indian stores.

Mirin Sweet Japanese rice wine. You can use dry sherry, sweetening it with 1 level teaspoon of caster sugar for each tablespoon of sherry.

Pomegranate syrup Can be bought in most Middle-eastern shops, but if you cannot find any you can prepare your own by boiling 225g (8 oz) sugar with 150ml (¼ pint) juice squeezed from fresh pomegranates and 150ml (¼ pint) water. Simmer gently for 20–30 minutes, strain, bottle and refrigerate until needed.

Santan coconut milk. Can be bought in tins, or you can make your own following the recipe on page 251.

Saké Japanese rice wine. You can use dry sherry as a substitute.

Sumac The dried crushed berries of a species of the sumach tree. It has a sour, lemony taste. Sumac can be bought from Middle-eastern, Indian and some Continental shops.

Tahina An oily paste made from roasted sesame seeds, available from Greek and Middle-eastern shops and often wholefood shops.

Terasi Indonesian dried shrimp paste. Use Chinese shrimp paste (*Belachan*) or shrimp sauce instead.

Urd dhal Skinned and split beans. If you cannot find this variety you can substitute any type of lentil.

Index

Arto der Haroutunian
Middle Eastern Cookery £2.95

Arto der Haroutunian, born in Syria and now living and cooking in England,
has collected recipes and ideas from family and friends in many Middle Eastern
countries for this wide-ranging introduction to the region's soups and salads,
pilafs, kebabs, casseroles and grills, from as far north as the Georgian
plains, from Afghanistan, from the hot deserts of Lebanon, Persia and
Armenia. The book is enriched by fragments of history, anecdote and fable
that accompany an unequalled collection of recipes to delight every lover of
good food.

Rita G. Springer
Caribbean Cookbook £2.95

Rita Springer, a leading expert on every aspect of Caribbean food, presents
a whole spectrum of mouthwatering recipes, reflecting the influence of
European, American and Chinese food as well as the traditional recipes of
the islands. Includes a chapter on Caribbean kitchen equipment, a helpful
glossary, and details of how to obtain the more unusual ingredients from
British suppliers.

'Exciting cooking' SUN

Carol Bowen
The Food Processor Cookbook £2.95

Chop, slice, grate, mix, blend, purée, mince – you name it, a food processor does it. As more and more people discover the magic of these versatile machines here is the book that helps you to save as much time and effort as possible *and* produce original and delicious dishes. Carol Bowen gives a complete rundown of the different types of processors available and she has provided a selection of mouthwatering recipes to put them to their best use.

The Microwave Cookbook £2.95

Microwave cooking means fast, efficient cooking. This book has proved an essential companion for microwave owners everywhere, and now it has been completely revised and updated to include an even wider range of practical tips, advice and recipe ideas. Including how to look after your microwave and get the best results from it. Plus quick reference charts to give cooking times for a wide variety of foods.

Kenneth Lo
Quick and Easy Chinese Cooking £1.95

Master the art of Chinese cooking the easy way under the guidance of top
cook and food writer Kenneth Lo. He's selected over 200 recipes for you
to try, all of them simple to prepare and ready in minutes. Useful sections
on menu-planning and combining dishes help you to achieve that authentic
Chinese flavour. Chinese cooking is fun – here's how to enjoy it to the full.

Dorothy Hall
The Book of Herbs £1.95
The unique flavours, perfumes, oil and mineral supplies and antiseptic
properties of herbs have made them indispensable as aids to health and
well-being for centuries. In this complete and thorough guide, Dorothy Hall
shows you how to grow herbs and how to use them in cooking, for health
and beauty, for improvement of the soil, to control garden pests – and even
as snuff and tobacco.

Cook books

☐ **Mrs Beeton's Cookery For All**	Mrs Beeton	£3.95p
☐ **The Microwave Cook Book**	Carol Bowen	£2.50p
☐ **Pressure Cooking Day by Day**	Kathleen Broughton	£2.50p
☐ **Middle Eastern Cookery**	A. der Haroutunian	£2.95p
☐ **Vegetarian Cookbook**	Gail Duff	£3.50p
☐ **Crockery Pot Cooking**	Theodora Fitzgibbon	£1.50p
☐ **The Book of Herbs**	Dorothy Hall	£1.95p
☐ **Diet for Life**	Mary Laver and Margaret Smith	£2.50p
☐ **Herbs for Health and Cookery**	Claire Loewenfeld and Philippa Back	£2.50p
☐ **The Preserving Book**	Caroline Mackinlay	£4.50p
☐ **The Book of Pies**	Elisabeth Orsini	£1.95p
☐ **Learning to Cook**	Marguerite Patten	£2.75p
☐ **Wild Food**	Roger Phillips	£5.95p
☐ **The Complete International Jewish Cookbook**	Evelyn Rose	£2.95p
☐ **Caribbean Cookbook**	Rita Springer	£2.50p
☐ **The Times Cookery Book**	} Katie Stewart	£3.50p
☐ **Shortcut Cookbook**		£1.95p
☐ **Freezer Cookbook**	Marika Hanbury Tenison	£1.95p

All these books are available at your local bookshop or newsagent, or can be ordered direct from the publisher. Indicate the number of copies required and fill in the form below   12

....

Name_____
(Block letters please)

Address_____

_____

Send to CS Department, Pan Books Ltd, PO Box 40, Basingstoke, Hants
Please enclose remittance to the value of the cover price plus:
35p for the first book plus 15p per copy for each additional book ordered
to a maximum charge of £1.25 to cover postage and packing
Applicable only in the UK

While every effort is made to keep prices low, it is sometimes
necessary to increase prices at short notice. Pan Books reserve
the right to show on covers and charge new retail prices which
may differ from those advertised in the text or elsewhere